THE ILLEGALITY OF LYING AND FORBIDDEN FICTION

GREGORY HEARY

Once Upon a Time,..............In a time which never existed in all of history.

Basically, a fictional story is a lie because the time of the setting never existed and the events described never happened. But isn't it just for fun? Isn't it good to have imagination and fantasy? Well, it depends if you mean imagination or creativity. Creativity is very different than imagination. Before analyzing the effects of fiction, we have to examine the causes. Why does the vast genre of fiction exist?

Whenever someone writes a book they have a reason for it. Trust me with the amount of work involved in writing a book and then editing and editing and editing nobody writes books for the fun of it. While it is exhilarating to write, if there is no specific reason for someone to write then they won't have the motivation to finish. So why in the world would someone spend so much time and effort to write or tell stories in other formats, whether audio or video, about things which never happened? It could be for money, fame, credentials, egotism or any other base selfish reason. However, there are many other potential motivations. People could write for religious reasons, romantic reasons, political reasons, psychotic reasons or for self-esteem reasons. Although primarily an author will write because they want to have a social impact and influence on individuals who read their book which then leads to having an influence on society. Many authors want to change the way people think and act, for better or worse. I'm no different. I would like to hope I'm writing to please my Creator and doing a deed which will benefit me while I'm in the grave but as a secondary reason I also desire to influence society by enjoining what is good and forbidding what is evil so that the world I live in can be a better place in the present and future. At least I'm straightforward about it. However, a non-fiction writer has a much more difficult task for influencing society than a fiction writer does. This is because when you read a non-fiction book such as this, you know that I'm a human being who is communicating some information directly to you, so you have a certain level of social awareness making you less likely to be persuaded by what you read. With fiction on the other hand, most oftentimes the author veils themselves and their message behind imaginary characters. Usually fiction is an intentional means to teach someone something without them knowing that you were teaching them, thus an entertaining distraction is concocted to make the reader emotionally attached to the story so their intellectual guard goes down. At the end of the fictional tale there may be a certain lesson that is easy to identify, but from beginning to end there are many more lessons and doctrines being propagated that are not easily identified because they are disguised as plot details or character dialogue. One such example would be the famous story of the tortoise and the hare. Now most people can easily grasp that the lesson taught in the folktale is about putting forth one's best effort regardless of the circumstances and how consistency pays off in the end. What people don't catch is that it also teaches things about racism, drugs and sexuality.

Consider the Hare or the rabbit, which has been known since the time of antiquity to be a symbol of fertility and excessive sexuality, he is in direct competition or in contrast to the infertile turtle who is slow to reproduce and usually exercises monogamy. The rabbit gets a fast head start but eventually misses the reward at the end, whereas the slow-paced turtle implies that having sexual activity slowly is more rewarding and gets more accomplished at the end. That this interspecies race is known as a "race" cannot be ignored. Because the two racers are of different races of animals who just so happen to be of different colors. Realistically I don't think a tortoise can speak to a rabbit since they speak different languages and make different sounds which the other may or may not be able to hear. The lesson of the racing event opposes Darwin's theory of "survival of the fittest" because the fittest rabbit was defeated by the least fit turtle despite what the animal kingdom thought would happen. The story also symbolizes performance enhancing drugs that replace hard work as similar to the rabbit's natural talent and speed, however the tortoise who is consistent with stamina wins in the end thereby stressing that success depends on how much effort you exert instead of how productive you actually are. Thereby teaching a false concept of working harder getting better results than working smarter. All these life lessons are learned when a child hears about the tortoise and the hare who had their mythical race, but these lessons are disguised because it's a fictional story. Yet because it's a fictional story the child and their parents are more relaxed and encouraging of it being learned not realizing that this story will greatly affect the reader's morality/lifestyle on a subconscious level as it's designed to.

Now that is just one small example of how there are many subtle teachings contained within a short narrative. Now imagine if the tortoise and the hare story were hundreds of pages long instead of just a couple paragraphs. Or if it were a series spread into multiple books and movies, how many lessons would there be in such a lengthy tale? This is why every single scene in a fictious story has to be treated as a separate story. Because that is what it is, the author made up a bunch of stories and tied them together with similar characters to convey a main theme as well as obfuscate and hide the many and often much more important smaller themes contained throughout. As they say "The devil is in the details". Well, the real lessons the creators of fiction want people to learn are in the details that are not relevant to the overarching plot of the story. Think about it, why would the author write an extra paragraph of fiction if it didn't contribute to the storyline in any way? It is because while the paragraph may not matter to the fictional storyline, it is actually extremely important to the messages the fiction author wants to get across to their unsuspecting audience.

Fiction automatically lowers our natural intellectual guard making the exposed consumer more susceptible to intellectual indoctrination or brain pollution/contamination.

A real-life example of the effects fiction has was evident when I accompanied my mother to one of her book club events. First, as an avid reader I asked her why these people get together, what types of books do they read and who are they. I was told that many were retired English teachers and one of them was once a mayor. Thus I correctly concluded that these people were starved for attention and joined this book club so they could regain some of the lost spotlight which they missed having and feel some sense of social comfort. They tended to read popular fiction books that were entertaining and mainstream. This reconfirmed my guess that they were merely interested in being a social club and weren't concerned with the content of what they were reading. This is because when you read a book you are making an investment. You are investing your time, energy and most likely your money whether you purchased the book or if you spent money to obtain or borrow it. As with any investment the reason people read a book is to get some sort of return out of it, or profit. Ideally the return should be beneficial knowledge which helps you achieve your life goals or better equips you towards such achievements. However, fiction is usually an escape from reality. Although in reality it is much more sinister because every piece of literature is promoting a certain code of morality which influences its reader's thought process and subsequently the morality of society. Look at the effect Shakespeare had on societal standards. When he put out the play "Romeo and Juliet" it was shockingly scandalous. Dating was relatively unknown in the world at that time, as was suicide due to romantic stress. But as Shakespeare's play was spread throughout the world today suicide and dating are considered normal things, this is because fictional stories such as Shakespeare's have normalized it. Shakespeare became the Shaikh of Sexual immorality spearheading a sexual revolution all via a fable of falsehood that he actually plagiarized from 5 other playwriters who had put on the same play which was published 121 years earlier before

Shakespeare. Shakespeare also stole from others when getting material for his other famous plays. Yet they call it "art" and he is seen as a English cultural hero. Yet factually it is only when a culture/society/nation has no good in it, primarily due to false religions which stunt the moral upbringing of the nation, because it is an evil society of villains that they must create fictional heroes for their moral lessons. Then they value their storytellers who create their heroes. I repeat only in a society of evil villains do they have an industry of fictional heroes because their society has no moral people in real life to learn from. Thus if you truly want to identify the bad people and bad nations, then just find out which societies produce the most fiction and you will clearly find and label devils and the devils' allies. It is said that the devil is the master of lies, well the genre known as fiction is the devil's invention. Heroic societies abolish fiction because they have true life heroes to learn from, devilish gangs promote the falsehood under the guise of "artistic freedom" and "imagination".

Regarding my experience at my mother's book club, shortly after I entered some lady told me to pay attention because there will be a test at the end. Of course, this was meant to be a joke but it revealed that these former English teachers were trying to reestablish their lost authority and feelings of power in an attempt to relive their past glory. So, I was intrigued to say the least. Then they began to comment on the book they were supposed to have read and I was horrified. But before I critique their frightening reaction to the fictional book, I will give a short summary of the plot. It is what I call a realistic fiction story. This is because the story took place on planet earth during a time period and setting that actually existed, the first World War. However as real as the setting was, the characters and the story were complete fantasy. These are the most dangerous types of fictional stories because it is easy for the reader to forget that the whole thing is entirely falsified make-believe. Yes, the first World War did happen, but the author of this particular book simply manipulates the factual setting of WWI into giving his nonsense credibility that it otherwise wouldn't have had if he had made his story take place on Neptune. Such books are particularly adept at discreetly teaching their readers lessons because the reader eventually gets confused as to what is fact and what is fiction with fantasy and reality blending and they get taken for a ride they may never recover from. Anyways the book was about a fictional WWI soldier who had a fictional romance story interspersed with fake WWI action that partially matched genuine WWI action.

One of the few men who was there started off the discussion saying how he liked the frequent cuss words and the shocking instance of the main character shooting and killing one of his own men who retreated from battle. He said he heard stuff like that happened, because the author said it happened and foreshadowed it, but he was surprised that the character actually had the nerve to do it. Right there I was floored. This guy just applauded war crimes committed by an imaginary character! First of all, the character in the book never existed, so anything this guy did in the book never really happened even if based upon semi-factual incidents. But right from the beginning of the book's discussion the human readers revealed that they had forgotten that the book they had read was 100% make-believe. The reason fiction is called make-believe is because it makes you believe things you didn't believe in before. In this instance it made this guy think that committing a war crime is ok because some imaginary character did it in a book and he wasn't condemned or punished as a result. Additionally, the vulgar obscene swear words, while they gave the illusion of realism were unnecessary for the author to include such profanity and the end result is that it polluted the language and vocabulary of all who read that book. At that point, during my mom's book club meeting I put ear plugs in my ears and quietly began to read the non-fiction book I had brought with me. Next, I overheard another person comment on the rampant alcohol and drugs which were used and consumed throughout the book, which they giggled gleefully when describing. Being what society considers a religious person I was appalled because my Islamic religion prohibits the consumption of alcohol and many other types of interactions with such a carcinogenic poison, and coincidentally the book club was meeting in a religious building at the time; where although it was a Christian building, their religion also expressly prohibited alcohol, or at least it used to. So there I was the youngest person in the room by decades listening to elderly people glorify something which God has expressly condemned through numerous revelations and prophets as illegal. I nearly burst out in rage wanting to tell them, *"Don't you know GOD HAS FORBADE INTOXICANTS! Are you promoting sin and glorifying evil? What is wrong with you people!"* But instead, I just got up and left the room so I would not be in their wretched company. Unfortunately, even in another room, with earplugs in my ears I could still hear what they were saying. The other man continued by praising the sexual content of the fictional romance and how titillating it was, although he did manage to say it seemed a little unrealistic the way the woman acted when seducing the main character. He also thought it was a bit farfetched that the two were able to reunite after the war and he cited plot holes saying how he thinks it would've been impossible for them to have met up again. At this point my fury rose as they were reveling in fictional fornication, which is another major sin in most religions. It became clear by then that the effect of this particular book was to corrupt the morality of society and it had a satanic agenda even if the author was unaware of it. It was also funny to hear counterarguments from people saying how it is entirely reasonable to believe that the characters in the book were able to meet again even though they were both in such extreme circumstances. I almost laughed because it seemed nobody in the whole book club was aware of the fact that these two romantic lovers they are debating about never existed and they never actually met at any time since it was a fictional story, so of course it seems a little unbelievable because the author completely made the whole thing up out of thin air. For 10 minutes, as a group they went back and forth arguing about whether it was realistically possible for the characters to meet again while being oblivious to the reality that they never existed. It was sad because they were so engrossed in the filthy story of the author's fiction so much that they had forgotten it was fiction because it was set during WWI. Since WWI actually happened they would cite the war statistics to justify their positions on matters that were fictitious. In essence they were using real life statistics to argue about fantasy land. Eventually some astute women expressed her displeasure with the women in the book being portrayed as sexual objects. I thought, "*No duh! You're surprised that a misogynist man wrote a book with female characters that aren't real and he didn't accurately portray them as real women are. Maybe they don't seem like real women because they're not real women and they are just a figment of the author's perverted imagination!*" By that time I realized this whole book was at best pointless, but sadly it was damaging the mental outlook of its readers. Many of them no doubt internalized such portrayals as to how women are supposed to be and would then treat women as they were treated in the book as sexual objects under the delusion that it was proper because it was proper to do so in the book. While since the book's setting was during the highly religiously themed Christian inter-denominational Crusade often labeled as World War 1 it also made any reader think that the way the imaginary people in the book treated each other was the actual way people acted back then. Thereby slandering an entire generation of humanity and effectively rewriting history, culture and morality in the minds of the readers. Just when I thought it couldn't get any worse the people in the book club discussed what they thought of the ending with the character suddenly dying. Now to me it was pretty obvious why the sudden surprise death ending of the main character, the author simply had to end the book and didn't want to write a sequel so he ended the story by ending the main character. Although these people in the book club seemed to be deluded into thinking that this fictional story was real. Some thought it was tragic and goes to show that life sucks or that it is so sad that the guy died at such a young age thereby preventing him from enjoying life with his belusted. I was disgusted at these elder adults attempting to get a lesson out of something that never happened. The end result was that these people wasted over an hour of their lives discussing something that never took place, in which they glorified many different sins, gave a stamp of approval on all manners of immoral and criminal behavior, approved sexism, alcoholism, unjustified violence and all kinds of wickedness. As if that weren't bad enough, they then voluntarily tried to glean some kind of actionable lesson from this lurid tale which they could use in their daily life. That they considered things their religion said was sinful to be permissible made them disbelievers according to my religion and theirs too, so that was a bad enough influence I thought. Yet they were so attached that they sought to gain some kind of benefit from fantasy as if the author were trying to teach them some vital life lesson. Some people even began to think God was unjust for causing such an early death. Some even thought that the characters in the book might have happiness in the afterlife. In summary the effect this fictional story had was to make the people believe in a satanic morality in nearly every aspect of life and to disbelieve in God and root for the enemies of God by sympathizing with fictional disbelieving sinners who were unrepentant. But it gets even worse. The author of this fictitious story in real life committed suicide by blowing his brains out with his own shotgun! Now personally when I hear someone killed themselves, for me I tend to reject them wholesale because it is well known that people who commit suicide go to hell forever, I don't care if its Socrates, Vincent Van Gogh or whoever. Someone who killed themselves is not someone I think should be given attention or followed. Just in case you think I'm making up this rant on fiction with a fictitious example, the author of the fictious book this book club discussed is very famous and widely read throughout the world today. The author's name was Ernest Hemingway.

His evil fiction sadly outlives him earning him extra sins to be punished for in his grave, increasing his torment.

This pertains to a common problem people have with fiction. Many automatically assume that the lesson is good and that the author is a good person who if their lesson is obeyed it will lead you to heaven, even if they know the author is not good in any way. Many people think that a bad guy is capable of writing a good book. They aren't. Yes, a bad guy could write an entertaining book, but if there is no goodness in the guy then how can they possibly put goodness down on the pages? The sad reality is that authors of fiction are liars who will lead you to hell. The very definition of fiction is falsehood. It is impossible to teach something good by means of doing something bad. For example, violently beating one's spouse so they apologize for insulting you in front of your kids is not going to teach your kids that it is wrong to insult people. Doing bad things teaches bad things. Just like stealing or gambling in order to get money to give in charity will not teach someone to give charity nor will it be a good deed. Likewise lying about things by making up a story cannot possibly teach a good lesson overall. The end result no matter what "benefits" come about do not justify the means of lying via fictional story-telling.

To easily identify what messages the author of fiction has conveyed just examine the effect the story has upon the readers or consumers. Ask the audience what they thought about the story and what it was about. Then as they share their opinion ignore the plot of the tale and focus on the actions of its characters and view the fictional characters as though the author just told the reader this is how you should act in real life. With such an approach you will be able to see what the effect such characters had upon the reader/audience even if they don't realize the impact themselves. This is because humans tend to be imitative beings who follow others willingly or unwillingly. Realistically nearly every fictional character portrayed on TV and in movies are psychopaths. One reason so many people are so messed up is because when you repeatedly watch psychopaths in movies and on TV then the viewer interprets those fictional psychopaths as "not that bad" and then imitation of those characters is unavoidable. Next thing you know everyone will be harming themselves and people will say it's normal because everyone is doing it and the people on TV are even worse. That's the destructive power of mob mentality and the majority opinion of democracy. If something is wrong it's wrong, no matter if the whole world is doing it, saying it's right making it legal. Likewise if something is right it's right even if all the world is saying it's wrong making it illegal. And lying is wrong even if people have entertainment through it via fictional stories.

This is why God has sent us prophets and told us their stories factually via divine revelation accessed through his prophets, so we can follow prophets as examples rather than God make every single person into a prophet with personal revelation. Humans naturally seek role models to follow and mimic in their lifestyles and behaviors. As a species we are designed to follow examples from exemplary characters. So, what do you think exposure to imaginary characters will have on a human? They will imitate humanesque figments of imagination which were created by people with deplorable morals who do devilish deeds following and promoting evil religions. For someone to ever create fiction in itself one has to compromise the truth of reality and willingly tell lies. You cannot create fiction or consume fiction without accepting a false premise and lies as being legal before you begin the journey into fantasy land. If everyone agreed it was forbidden to tell anything other than the truth then fiction would not be able to be created. Fiction only exists in a world that legalizes lies. Truthfully global poverty, homelessness and starvation only exists today because of idiots spending money on fiction. God's prophets encouraged us to give charity to the needy, but we as a species need fantasy so much we value it over fulfilling the needs of needy humans.

Before any lesson can be learned from fiction it requires one to agree that it is ok to lie and make stuff up in the first place. So you have to do a bad deed before you can even create the work of fiction. By enjoying a work of fiction one is saying that lying a legitimate form of communicating. Also a creator of fiction is imitating God because God has created everything. In the fictional world the author is the creator of the characters and much more. Essentially a creator of fiction becomes the God of their own fantasy land. Because that fantasy land is inevitably different from the real world the real God made, they are putting forth the idea that they can make something better than God has. Why else would they try to teach a lesson using imaginary characters? We have the prophets as role models, we don't need imaginary characters to learn a single thing from. The imaginary characters are not going to paradise so they cannot possibly help you to go to paradise. So if they cannot teach you or motivate you to go to paradise then imaginary characters can only teach you evil and lead you to hell. Fiction is the genre of Satan and it leads to toleration of false religions and lies and all other sorts of ills and evils that plague our species. Fiction desensitizes us to sins and crime rates have increased in direct proportion to fiction proliferation.

Before any lesson can be learned from fiction it requires one to agree that it is ok to lie and make stuff up in the first place. So, you have to do a bad sinful deed before you can even write/film or read/watch the work of fiction. To accept the existence of a work of fiction is to accept lying falsehood as being okay. By reading a work of fiction one is making lying a legitimate form of communicating so there is guaranteed harm that outweighs any alleged benefit. Seriously a creator of fiction is saying, *"I'm going to tell lots of lies to tell a story, but there's a good reason for me to make all this fake stuff up. Just listen to my many lies and enjoy learning."* Whereas personally a good person would just stop the fiction fabricator right there and say, *"No! Don't lie. Tell me what you want without telling me any lies. If you have to tell a lie to tell me what you want then don't because to tell the lies is sinful. So, I'm not interested in your fiction because I want the truth and hate lies and liars."* Personally, I wouldn't even read fiction if it were assigned in school unless it were to analyze and expose the religious doctrines and lessons taught by the author both plainly and subliminally. But is that what teachers and students do in school when they consume works of fiction? Do they treat it as a detective would trying to identify the lies and evil doctrines spewed by the fiction maker? Typically not. Instead the teachers foolishly tend to try to make the student think about the psychology of the fictional characters and their motivations as if they were real people, thereby the teachers try to make the students identify with the characters thinking it will better help them with interpersonal and communication skills in life or gain new perspectives or culturally assimilate. Yet the characters aren't real and were just made up by the fiction maker to teach people certain things without them knowing it and identifying/sympathizing with the characters is exactly how the things intending to be subliminally taught are taught. Most who "study a work of fiction" are imbibing its hidden doctrines even moreso than the one just enjoying it for fun without studying it. For example, when was the last time a teacher teaching a work of fiction ever told their student, "*Why do you think this author would just lie and make up this character and portray them in such a way doing these things which they never did? What do you think the author wants you to believe and do after learning about this character?*" Sadly, nearly zero teachers do this because they simply don't know how to teach, they are simply professional indoctrinators without knowing it because they've been indoctrinated themselves to teach a doctrine they don't even know they are teaching when they teach things. Hence I say most kids who go to most schools exit as a fool that has been trained to be a tool to be used to serve the desires of those they won't even know are benefitting by their labor and play when they labor and play. Hence fiction is a subgenre of religion in which every author of fiction teaches their own faith. Also a creator of fiction is blasphemously imitating God because God has created everything. Fiction is the genre of Satan and it leads to toleration of false religions and lies and all other sorts of ills and evils that plague our species. While I have focused mainly on written works of fiction the same applies to fictional movies, songs, news broadcasts, plays, operas, tv shows, videos, games, skits etc. All these are works of fiction that have the same result and negative immoral influences on those that are affected by them or interact with those contaminated by them. What is the proof that all works of fiction are satanic productions, aside from the fact that fiction is an entre of lies? Well look at the fundamental lesson taught by every work of fiction. What lesson is that? The fundamental lesson in fiction is so obvious you should be ashamed to not have seen it. If you haven't already guessed what it is, then it shows that you have been thoroughly brainwashed by the genre of fiction. Do you really not know the overarching theme of fiction? The ever so popular fictional worlds and tales of fantasy land take God and the prophetic religion out of the picture entirely. Consider the role the prophetic religion plays in fictional tales. How many times do the characters pray every day? How often do the characters mention the prophets or their authentically transmitted teachings and cite them as examples to help them know what the best course of action is? The overwhelming majority of fictional stories don't even contain the word "God" let alone give any significant importance to God in their fictional universe. Therein lies the fundamental goal of fiction: to make people believe in a world free from God and the perfect prophetic religion of Islam. Consider the heroes of the fictional tales, typically their religion is self-made and they act as though they are their own prophet making their own rules to life as if somehow that's okay. This desensitizes people to be disillusioned with religious legal systems as viable or applicable. Whereas if you use God's criteria, if you were to take all the fictional characters that have ever existed, more than 99.9% of them would burn in hell forever. Yet at the end of a thrilling fictional story how often are you left thinking all the characters you just learned about will burn in hell forever and are wicked people hated by God? Never, instead one is left sympathetic to these fictional devils and will most likely apply more lessons learned from that fictional story than they will true lessons the prophets of God taught. In sum the fiction genre portrays people God labels bad as good. By being exposed to fiction you begin to believe that those God would hate are good people to learn from or imitate. Basically, fiction causes people to sympathize with the forces of Satan and acclimate to a world without God or the prophetic religion. The effect of most fiction being that you waste countless hours of your life to get less religious while watching/reading something wherein you don't think of God for a single second. Which if you recall is exactly what Satan wants you to do with your life. So some might claim fiction is just fun, but in reality fiction interrupts one's relationship with God and makes you forget your Creator despite your Creator never forgetting you and having angels record all you do for your court date on Judgement Day. While even the rare religiously themed fiction is poison because it justifies the genre and makes people think it's okay to lie which is the exact opposite of what the prophetic religion teaches. The prophetic religion forbids fiction and lying so how then can one possibly teach the prophetic religion by doing something the religion says is forbidden? Simply put one can't even if one intended to, and that's why the prophets never promoted fiction. The prophets of God unanimously actually forbid all fiction as a form of false testimony or lying. It was the sinful practice of the polytheistic Greeks and Romans who developed fictional entertainment. Fiction was sinful then and will always remain to be so even if disguised in garments of religious fiction or spiritual acting.

Another reason fiction is destructive is because it is a closed circuit. Learning information from a fictional story will not benefit you in any aspect of life outside of that fictional fantasy. If you read one fictional book from one author and another fictional book from another the previous book does not help you or enhance the 2nd book you read. In comparison every non-fiction book improves your future experiences reading non-fiction books because the information carries over. For example, I may read about a certain historical event in a non-fiction book in depth. Next, I read another non-fiction book that makes a comment referring to that historical event I read about in the other book. Due to previously reading the first non-fiction book and knowing about the event the second book mentioned then my understanding of the second book is greatly enhanced and improved as a result. What is even more amazing is that the author of the second book had no idea that I would have such knowledge to be able to benefit in such a way from their brief comment. So by me reading non-fiction books it makes non-fiction books I read in the future more informative and beneficial than they would have been if I had not read the other non-fiction books in the past. Therein lies innumerous benefits that carry over from one book to the next in a never-ending series of non-fiction books. Essentially all of the world's non-fiction books belong to the same series and you can read the series in any order you want without being out of the loop. With non-fiction it also keeps you in the realm of the real world. Therefore the person is not using such non-fiction as an escape outlet into a virtual reality world. The consumer of non-fiction is better able to develop mentally, emotionally and spiritually because they are consistently dealing with reality. They are never deluded into pretending life is different than what it is. Thus they can improve themselves and their society because they are familiar with reality and problem solving in the real world. The solutions in fictional stories do not work in the real world, else you would find them in non-fiction. Every book you read and everything you do should help you become a better person, fiction doesn't help you become a better person. How can you possibly gain a good moral lesson from characters that never existed in a setting that never existed doing things that never really happened? You can't get a lesson from something that didn't happen, learn your morality from reality. If your morality comes from fantasy then your morals are fictitious. God created us to be in this world for a specific reason. By pretending and concerning ourselves with an imaginary universe that doesn't exist we forget the reality of Heaven and Hell and that in a few moments we will be taken from this world into one of those places to reside therein forever.

At best you do not get any reward for spending time on fiction. Yet because that is a waste of the time with the body parts God has given you, spending time on frivolous fiction is actually a bad deed and sin, regardless of what the fiction is about. Know fully well that there is no such thing as "free time" where God will resurrect you on the Day of Judgement and say, *"Well you did this during "free time" so it doesn't count as either a good or bad deed, I won't judge you for what you did at that time of your life."* No time is free, every second of our short life will be examined and scrutinizingly judged by our Creator for goodness or evilness and those who choose the illusionary neutrality of mythological "free time" and theoretical permissible activities are losers bound to do evil even if they merely waste their lifespan. But fiction is not neutral by a longshot. Regarding fiction the whole work is based on lying, and frequently is extremely sinful in subject and content too. In reality, fiction is an addictive affliction on the planet that is actively destroying the moral fabric of society, stunting our development, making us susceptible to Satan and taking us away from God and the path to paradise. God created us to be in this world for a specific reason. Whatever you do you are making an investment of time and energy, so that investment better help you in this life and the next. Basically if the activity won't aid your journey to paradise in any way then you should not do it. Whenever you do something you have to have a intended goal. That goal must be religious in some aspect and it is religious even if the person isn't. This is because every activity ever done is very religious in multiple ways.

The most powerful people in the world today and throughout history have been readers of non-fiction. Napolean Bonaparte testified to this when he said: *"Show me a family of readers, and I will show you the people who move the world."* The solutions in fictional stories do not work in the real world, else you would find them in non-fiction. Fiction doesn't help you become a better person no matter what type of fiction it is. Ideally the return on your investment in any activity should be beneficial knowledge which helps you achieve your life goals or better equips you towards such achievement. Yet fiction is usually treated as an escape from reality, or something popular to consume or "study". Although in reality it is much more sinister because every piece of fiction is promoting a certain code of morality which influences its consumer's thought process and subsequently the morality of global society. At best you do not get any reward for spending time on fiction. Yet because that is a waste of the body parts God has given you as well as the time God has given you, then spending any time on frivolous fiction is actually a bad deed and sin, regardless of what the fiction is about. Whereas most fiction is sinful in subject and content as well. For instance, if you were to have two strangers come to your house and ask to come inside and be romantic in front of you and your family then what would you say? An honorable person would refuse to see such a display in their home, but when strangers are on TV or a movie is streamed in the home and they act romantic onscreen is the reaction to seeing illicit romance the same? How about if strangers came to your door asking you to listen to them utter profanities, tell crude immoral jokes, consume alcohol or do drugs or to commit acts of violence inside your home? Most would refuse such a face-to-face intrusion, but not when it's on a TV! Yet realistically what is the difference between strangers doing something immoral in your home in the flesh and actors/actresses doing it fictionally in your home in books, TV shows, movies and songs? The sin has still entered your home and heart degrading your religious character and worst of all some people find this mutual crime to be entertaining and pay money for it. Which makes it worse. Because if you paid random strangers on the street to come to your home to do the stuff fictional characters do on the stories you consume in your home, you would be hard pressed even in today's immoral society to find willing participants even for large sums of money. Which truly shows the moral depravity of actors and actresses. And even those immoral people put a hefty price on performing the lewdness the fictional tale requires them to do because it is known to be repulsive and scandalous to do, let alone be seen doing on a widespread scale. But worst of all, out of all the sins I mentioned you wouldn't allow done in your home by random people off the street, is that under the guise of fiction people allow the greatest sin of all. They allow religious disbelief to be done in their presence. Most religious people would not allow disbelievers or religious blasphemers or heretics to have a place in their homes. Yet when it's on TV or a fictional tale then somehow all their religious loyalty is lost. No longer do they love and hate only for the sake of their Lord, instead they open their soul up to unknown creators and characters of fiction to influence them as they deem fit. Fiction entirely eliminates religious allegiance because even if the characters are portrayed as all being from your religion, the actors and actresses themselves are otherwise. Likewise, from a Muslim perspective most fiction, as with TV for the most part, normalizes a niqab-free world; of which scholars have stated the niqab is obligatory for

Muslim women to wear in public in front of non-relatives according to the safest strongest opinion of the Salaf. Even if one follows the hijabi opinion, most fiction is set in a world where the hijab is not normal either. And then even when you have actresses wear hijab in pretend shows, it's not worn properly and the actors and actresses pretend to be relatives for the fictional story but in reality are not. So all their interactions with the other gender under the guise of acting are sinful under God's law. Religiously even outside of Islamic guidelines fiction stories deem modesty itself is not the normal way for the world to operate. So, every fictional tale essentially teaches you a dress code as well as religious doctrines. Never forget that fiction makes fashion statements too. Fiction from TV and other avenues has destroyed countless families and their values enslaving humans for generations. This is because turning on fiction, and for the most part TV in general, turns off growth and real-life self-development. People who value their lifespan don't waste their life on filth like forbidden fiction.

As a disclaimer some fiction can be "studied" to see its effects on the world but this is not for average people to do "for fun", nor for Scholastic students to do. Whereas that's the problem with schools and most "book clubs", in that they "study fiction" trying to analyze it not realizing it's just something somebody made up that is all a bunch of lies. It doesn't matter if it was Shakespeare or some other famous fiction maker, if it's fiction it's filthy garbage no matter how famous it is. Shakespeare is a scoundrel because he is a liar who made things up thus teaching people it was okay and fun to lie. That is the principal lesson of all works of fiction in that they all teach lying is permissible, and at that point they are wrong so one shouldn't even bother listening to anything else they have to say after that. Regardless, whether it's Shakespeare or someone with more literary dignity it is the epitome of stupidity to discuss fiction in a manner of "What do you think will happen next?" or "What do you think they did/happened to them after that?". I don't even tolerate people seriously discussing fiction around me, because it's too stupid to ignore. I'll interrupt and say, "*Are you discussing what fictional characters will do in a non-existent realm/timeline? Do you realize that those characters do not exist and their stories never happened? Why are you spending your time talking and thinking about characters who don't exist and possible activities that will never ever and could never ever occur? Do you realize none of that movie/tv show/book/comic was real and that stuff did not happen? Why are you talking about nonsense that non-existent characters never did in real life? If you want to discuss fiction, why don't you do it in the fictional world? Go back to fantasy land if you want to talk about fantasy, right now you are in reality so please act and think accordingly. Please change the setting on your brain and tongue to "real-life mode". Do you realize that in the real world all those fictional characters are villains trying to suck you out of reality to the poisonous realm of fantasy? Be a real-life hero and fight fiction so the fictional characters don't take over reality. The more attention you pay to fiction the more powerful they become. Those fictional fiends have enslaved you and taken real time from your real life. They feed on your time, thoughts and feelings. It is time to be liberated from them once and for all lest they destroy you and us all. Fight your fiction addiction and conquer it before it conquers you. They aren't real, the stories didn't happen. Don't waste your life!"*

Comedy tends to be an ally of fiction since so much comedy is based upon or involves fiction, so I give comedy a similar treatment as fiction in that if it's not real it's not funny and most comedy today is vulgar or sinful anyways built upon fictional scenarios. Now don't mistake this to mean one can't have fun reading, listening or watching things at all. Yet fiction and most comedy genres are wasteful and destructive to the intellect and morality of their indulgers. The only reason any scholar could ever justify studying fiction is to discern what false religious messages were disseminated by popular fictional tales so that people can be informed where they got their false ideas about religion, life and bad morals from. Fiction is highly influential. For example, the famous fictional "Christmas Carol" story published by Charles Dickens in 1834 CE described the villain "Scrooge" forcing his employee to work on Christmas. Many today think that's cruel, yet when Dickens wrote that story Christmas was an illegal holiday in America due to Puritan Colonial Christians banning it in all 13 original states. So everybody worked on Christmas, even the politicians, and in some states Americans would get fined if they celebrated Christmas. However, as a result of the popularity of Dickens' fictional fable, the state of Alabama in 1836 CE declared Christmas a legal holiday and other states followed until Oklahoma was the final state to legalize Christmas in 1907 CE. The American Federal Government made it a legal civil holiday in 1870 CE overturning hundreds of years of laws banning Christmas for having pagan and papal origins. Thereupon a fictional story ended up changing Christmas from an illegal holiday to a legal popular one. Now some might think that's good but whether it's good or bad is irrelevant. The point is fiction changes the world and it does so based on lies. It's because of our society tolerating peaceful fiction that we end up killing each other in really violent wars waged due to lies.

One look at today's newspapers and social networks is proof enough that the alleged Torah commandment given to Moses forbidding false testimony or false witness aka lying/fiction is rarely practiced. Lies upon lies upon lies are being accepted in courts as truthful eyewitness evidence. People get tortured, killed and go to war based on fraudulent testimony or skewed biased media. Hollywood films have flipped the script on many war-time facts turning war criminals into superstars. Many people say things they can't confirm not realizing the gravity of what it means if they guess wrong, or repeat a rumor that isn't true without specifying that it's a rumor.

People even sign documents with names other than their own or lie about the date a document was signed. Lies have become so prevalent in society that people even lie in order to tell jokes. Mistakenly believing that they're not sinful because it's "funny". Such lies of allegedly small sizes implies the liars don't find the truth funny. Which makes sense because God is not known for being a comedian. We shouldn't think the laws of God are mere jokes. Those who laugh at God's religion now won't be laughing later when the hellfire asks God for more fuel. It's a very serious matter to spread false testimony. One joke containing false testimony could cause the joker to burn in the eternal hellfire. The creators of fiction are liars qualified for such punishment, so what then about those who enjoy their lies as "fun entertainment" who spend more time on fictional activities than the prophetic faith? Yet despite knowing that most television programs are forbidden due to the sins of fictional lying/acting, indecent dress codes, idle talk, music, lewd speech, anti-prophetic immoral teachings and actions glorifying disbelief in God and sinfulness as a way of life and serving as a waste of our precious lifespan, how many are willing to live life without television as a safety precaution? It is well-known how corrupting television is yet people persist on the poison citing miniscule chance of worldly benefit despite drowning in the sins of cinematography while at the same time such people think when the antichrist comes then he will be a minor challenge to them because their faith is so strong.

In reality if you got a television in your house, chances are you watch sinful stuff on it, and chances are that should the antichrist emerge you would fail the test because you can't even resist an opportunity to sin with television. Truly they need not worry about losing to the antichrist because the devil already beat them with a television or fiction of other formats. People are drowning in sin so much their heart grew gills from the virus called fiction.

If the world is to change for the better it has to be changed via telling the truth not by popular fictional falsehood. The ends alleged to be accomplished by fiction do not justify the means. Falsehood is what made the world a mess in the first place. Fairytales turned the real world into a nightmarish hellhole. So while the fiction itself should be ignored, the effects of fiction can be studied so as to learn from the ways fiction influenced us so as to diminish the effects fiction has on the world in the present and future. Consider fiction like drugs, you study the drugs to learn how to rid the world of them but you don't ingest the drugs yourself. Like drugs, frequently the fiction addiction blinds the junkie to the negative side effects of fiction, while those who know of the dangers of fiction abstain from it. Whereas studying comedy is a joke because most of the jokes are only funny if you have corrupt morals. Comedy has less of an influence in society but is more of a supplement to other things that influence society. Laypeople should ignore fiction so the wicked cycle of lies can stop and scholars can focus on fixing real-world problems. Comedy can be useful to employ if it is done naturally for a good purpose but it's not a hobby or a valid interest. Comedy itself teaches many religious messages more easily because it makes things funny when they could be sinful or not funny. Prophets weren't comedians and not a single companion of a prophet was known to be a funny full-time joker. Prophets didn't hang around people who told lots of jokes constantly because real life isn't that funny, making things in life funny all the time is a type of fiction. Comedy can be a powerful gateway to fiction. That's why Satan usually starts with a joke to make you comfortable in life before teaching you to sin and disbelieve. Satan starts with comedy and gets the last laugh when you die as a sinful disbeliever due to laughing through life as if God created you to giggle. God lets you giggle when it's appropriate but we are in the middle of a spiritual war against Satan so laughter can't cause us to leave our guard down, let alone befriend liars. Both Fiction and Comedy also teach religious doctrines.

Music is no different but it is vastly more dangerous. Regarding Poetry the Quran in chapter 26 verses 221 – 227 says what in English means:

Shall I inform you upon whom the devils descend? (221) They descend upon every sinful liar. (222) They pass on what is heard, and most of them are liars. (223) And the poets - [only] the deviators follow them; (224) Do you not see that in every valley they roam (225) And that they say what they do not do? - (226) Except those [poets] who believe and do righteous deeds and remember Allah often and defend [the Muslims] after they were wronged. And those who have wronged are going to know to what return they will be returned. (227)

And what is music without rhythm and rhymes? This Quranic condemnation is about plain poetry without music accompanying it. Most poetry is fictitious spoken by liars as is most music. The poets and musicians lie in order to complete their rhymes because most of the time the truth doesn't rhyme, nor does it sell well. Regarding poetry, the authentic hadith reported by Abu Huraira in Sahih Bukhari 6155 shares that Prophet Muhammad taught: *"It is better for anyone of you that the inside of his body be filled with pus which may consume his body, than it be filled with poetry."*

Again, this is regarding poetry alone without instrumental accompaniment. So, if poetry vocals or written poetry alone is worse than feeding upon pus, then what about having a song stuck in your head, or entire songs memorized, or entire playlists of musical albums rolling around inside your head and heart? Especially when they are a type of fiction on top of the sin of musicality? Music is basically a list of recited lies mixed with instruments. And I proclaim this as a former religious musician who prior to Islamic guidance made allegedly good religious music or so I foolishly claimed. In actuality my music was religious as everything is, but it is impossible to spread the prophetic faith through sins such as music. Sadly, I unintentionally and regretfully made satanic polytheistic aka Christian music in the name of prophetic characters like Jesus. Despite the long history of Christian Scholars actually forbidding music themselves as sinful just as they used to forbid the sins of usury/interest and alcohol.

In the college where I obtained my Associate's Degree in Audio Recording and Production, the classes were mostly about music. Some taught musical history and development, some taught music as an art and some taught music as a science. However, the more important and technical training courses plainly taught that music is a drug. At first it sounded ludicrous, but there was no way to deny the scientific proof the professors presented to prove their thesis about music being an auditory drug. They taught us the way the ear is structured and how sound is processed and the effects music has on the brain, emotions, mentality and body. At first it seemed as though they had exposed a big secret, but inside we all knew music was a drug all along. Everyone exposed knows that music is more addictive than most drugs that have ever been created. Music is simply unforgettable. It is easier for your brain to forget chemical drug cravings than song lyrics and rhythms. Music is so powerful that you can go years without hearing a song, then you overhear it for 5 seconds by accident and the entire song comes back to your mind with you knowing all the lyrics by heart while your emotions time-travel back to how you felt when you used to listen to it. This type of experience is unparalleled and very dangerous. Imagine someone made a song you liked the sound of but it had some bad advice. By having your brain remember that song against your will that bad advice will be stuck in your head for the rest of your life. Who knows when your brain might act upon it without telling you where it got that idea from? Music is a drug according to the elite of the music industry and professors who train people how to create music professionally. The little kids like pop stars because the pop music is the gateway drug, everyone enjoys it their first time but when they develop a taste for a more refined composite intoxicant then pop music doesn't have that same buzz. The pop music is still intoxicating but those with more musical experience don't get the same high from the generic gateway drug of music as they do with the more dangerous compound varieties. People having different tastes in music is the same as people having different tastes regarding drugs. All forms of the drug type known as music are dangerous and intoxicating, they just have different flavors and side effects with some being more damaging or addictive than others. As a former music junkie who used to listen to over 8 hours of music daily, trust me when I say that music is not something you want to get hooked on. Music will damage your hearing, poison your mind, corrupt your heart and take control over your life without you even realizing it. If you do listen to music there is a 99.99% chance you will be enslaved to melodious rhythm and brainwashed by the musicians. Second-hand smoke is actually less likely to affect you than music. Some genres of music even qualify as religions. Such as Hip-Hop which has a code of conduct and a Hip-Hop Gospel taken as Scripture and even official Temples dedicated to the religion of Hip-Hop. If people knew what a fraud the musician's lifestyle was like they wouldn't put them on a pedestal or even respect them. Devastatingly, the listeners will often believe whatever they hear and only see what the musician desires them to see. Many of the musicians actually think this deception of people is funny. It is sickening to know that some musicians secretly laugh at their fans in private because the fans have been fooled into thinking the artist is what they pretend to be. Don't be fooled by the publicity stunts, smoke and mirrors or by what you hear. Don't fall for the expensive fictional optical and auditory illusions musicians create. All musicians are actors to satanic scripts, even moreso the religiously themed performers who preach via the innovative method of using music.

Difference in music quality is like graphic design, if two people have an idea for a picture their ideas don't really make much difference as to which picture will be better it depends primarily on the technology. For instance, the one who draws their picture on a cave wall is going to have a lower quality product than the one using the latest graphic design computer software, regardless of what their ideas and talents were. The technology trumps everything when manufacturing music. Therefore the more money that is spent on making music the higher the quality regardless of whether the artist is talented or not. So, when people say a certain artist is bad, many times it simply means they have a low budget and the listener isn't used to listening to music made with that type of budget. Money can make terrible artists sound great and lack of money can make elite artists sound terrible. High quality music is not priceless, it's just out of the price range of most people. Therefore the artist is marketed as if they were a brand-named product. As part of increasing business they must spend on their public image, namely give the impression they're getting rich off of music because then the public will psychologically think their music is good because they seem and claim to get so much money for it.

The richer they appear the more people will think they make, and the better a musician they become in the public's eyes the better they will sound to the public's ears. Hence the musicians spend lavishly on jewelry and such stuff to boost their image in order to gain more customers in order to spend money on their brand. This creates a cycle of spending money on music and promotion to make money on music to spend money on music and promotion without ever really making any genuine money unless they get to an extremely high level where they can use that celebrity status as a source of revenue through other means outside of music. Most all of the money an artist makes goes into promoting themselves. So in order to cut costs they will wear fake jewelry and rent things for music videos and photoshoots. Those who do spend lavishly on themselves aren't getting that money exclusively from selling music and if they are then by spending promotional funds on fun stuff they risk their musical product falling behind the quality of the other competitors; which is why you have one-hit wonders. The "one-hit wonder" is the person who didn't spend enough money on their next song and promotion but spent it on other things. Hit songs are easy to make, songs are "hits" simply because of familiarity and people listen to a song because it's what they routinely expect to hear. Music junkies will listen to a song they "don't like" or even one they "hate" because it's familiar and they can sing along. A "hit" is just a formulaic song which a music junkie can't resist. New songs can be purposefully made into popular hit songs by radio stations if they just play the new song after and before other popular songs, thereby making a "hit sandwich" where the middle meat of a new song placed between two loaves of hit songs causes the new song to be considered as a bread and butter hit. It's really that easy, in reality people do not even have a choice whether a song becomes a viral hit song or not. The musical industry is purely a financial business. Anyone can be a star with enough money spent on their music and promotion, the only thing is whether that particular brand name product can turn a profit for the corporate record labels who decide to sell them as a product. The music industry is basically like prostitution, some prostitutes have a pimp and some don't. The merchandise rendered from both is the same, the only difference is the amount of money spent on the promotion and healthcare as well as customers having different tastes. Just as the sex addict has more expensive tastes than those less experienced, the music addict doesn't find the same pleasure from the less expensive music so they will oftentimes supplement their addiction with quantity once their taste in quality has plateaued. Although unlike with prostitution the musical technology continues to advance in sophistication much faster than typical drug potency increases. Music is a special type of drug in which there is no "rock bottom" possible because the music industry continues to increase the potency of its drug along with the rapid technological advancements. The only catch is that the musical technology upgrades so fast, the musical junkies can't keep up with the increased potency which is why many old folks who love music don't care for the new music because in audio terms it's too complex and potent for their system to handle. Most older folk get a musical overload which triggers an audio effect similar to a drug overdose which is why they will say "That ain't music!" just like a drug user will say about a drug they can't handle "That ain't no drug!" Whereas the young music junkies who grew up on the more complex musical drugs will hardly get a buzz from the old music, unless a particular song was specifically associated with an emotional feeling or timeframe so that it triggers nostalgia for them. This is because whether a person likes or dislikes a particular song is based on the amount of mental effort it takes for them to listen to it. The less resistance the brain has to a song then the greater the tolerance for that song will be and the more it can be enjoyed or used to get a buzz. Yet because of the personal nature of music, it's not quite the same as a mere drug, because drugs typically don't have much to do with their manufacturers or dealers, whereas music is intimately related to their manufacturers and dealers. Music has the elements of emotional drugs as well as the elements of physical drugs while being a mental drug with a unique auditory injection system that can in theory never be blocked by attempts to detox since our hearing cannot be turned off, nor can our hearing be shut down via an overdose. As long as volume is kept within safe ranges and the stereocilia remain alive and the auditory brainwaves connect then there is no limit to how much one can indulge in music, they could even be taking it while they are sleeping. Therefore all these qualities make music the ultimate drug. However, because unlike other drugs music can be laced with ideas and messages, it can be used as a special category of propaganda that is extremely unique and influential beyond measure. For those with experience and training it's very easy to compose a melismatic rhythm with both conjunct and/or disjunct motion accompanied by various pitches to create a harmony or chord of consonance and/or dissonance that overwhelms the senses filling the body and brain with dopamine rendering the listener mindless and thereby susceptible to believe and act upon any suggestions they hear during the song. Those suggestions tend to be called lyrics with the instrumentals being the main compound which facilitates the lyrical dose of propaganda. Although the vocals can either be an integral layer of texture or in strophic format making them easily interchangeable and replaceable regardless of the tempo, dynamics, genre or form of music. Meaning the lyrics can be intoxicating by themselves without any accompanying instrumentals or they can have nothing to do with the musical composition and be 100% constructed without any attention as to how they will fit in with the music since the way some music is made can allow for literally any type of lyrics to be inserted and sound compatible, or the lyrics to a song can be both; or neither if the music is of poor quality. And by poor quality music, I mean it has less intoxicating effect, similar to how an alcoholic will say "X is a good brew and Y is a bad brew" even though it's still alcohol the quality is linked to intoxication ability and not necessarily the pleasure derived from flavor. Monophonic, Polyphonic, Imitative Polyphonic and Homophonic music all intoxicate the listener but on different unique levels. Think of those terms as Class A drug of music, Class B drug of music, Class C drug of music and Class D drug of music, the genre itself has minimal effect on intoxication and the different classes don't necessarily denote higher ability to intoxicate but they are just different classifications regarding the complexity of the compounds that are generally more intoxicating to those who use their ears to experiment or indulge with such sounds. No music can ever have its total impact measured or analyzed by humans. All types of music will "get you high" but in different ways and to different levels of intoxication. Some just get higher off certain musical drug classes more than others. The record labels are pimps and the artists are prostitutes, some musicians become their own pimps with varying results. The prostitute(musician) with a pimp(record label) will appeal to more people while the independent prostitute(musician) will usually have a smaller consumer base, yet their consumers will be more devoted because of the lack of the intermediary. Although with advances in social networking now those artists with pimps can easily attain the same close connection with their consumers as unsigned artists did in the past. The music industry is pure prostitution and those in the industry know it, the main difference is that it's legalized and primarily sells an auditory product or performance instead of a sexual encounter. Any who are in the industry and think they're different is just like the prostitute who doesn't want to face the fact they are a prostitute but claims to be an "artist". Many fans will think their favorite artist is the exception in the business, but I assure you there are no exceptions. Musicians are as fond of their fans as prostitutes or strippers are of their clientele. Just as the prostitute claims to really love their patron the musicians will say the same about their fans. Do some prostitutes genuinely fall in love with their clients? Yes, but it's a delusional narcissism based off the lust of the clients. Musicians love fans because the fans love their music. Also when making the drug of music, you get exposed to your own material during the creation and promotion process thereby getting high off of your own product, and it is even more powerful because you are making it so it's like tasting your own cooking; even if it has bad flavor it tastes good because of you making it. As a result, musicians can frequently become addicted to their own music and start to believe it. Meaning, they've smelled their own poop so much that they think it's tasty nutritious food which they eat and market to others. When that happens, and it is a when not an if, they have their music take over their life to the point where they are no longer creating the music but the music is creating the musician and they're addicted to it. Then a music junkie musician becomes their own drug dealer. While fans then become enablers to a music junkie encouraging them to make more of the drug they all use and glorify a musical drug dealer that gets high off his own supply. Which will either push the musician to make more and more of higher potency, using their musical drug to help them make stronger musical drugs or they get so high off their own music they crash and burn since they can't perform and maintain or increase their level of drug creativity nor quality. Exactly like the drug dealers on the street corners, all the musicians say they got the best supply on the market, except for those who are deeply addicted to other musicians since most of them are consumers before they are producers. Whereas the dream of the junkie musician then is typically to get rich and famous and influential making your own auditory drugs for your own consumption while getting a bunch of fans to cheer you on for doing it and love you for it; taking your own drugs like some type of hero. Some musicians even get called kings but they are drug kingpins, and for those called gods they are really druglords. It's an evil industry unlike any other ever known to mankind that heavily relies on fiction for fuel, as people rarely ever fact check songs for honesty.

The lifestyle of a musician is actually anti-religious and they are given far too much undeserved influence. Music itself creates false desires and emotions also causing one to reminisce. Many songs are technically prayers and can make their listeners disbelievers if they recite the lyrics. If you hear them over and over again subconsciously you'll start thinking like the singers. Music is a drug too dangerous to be using which is impossible not to abuse, or come under the influence of, if it is heard. Why do you think movie production companies spend millions of dollars to include just a couple of songs in a movie? They do this because the music is more important than the plot and the acting. A movie can have a bad story or acting performance, but well-placed music can make a memorable classic.

If you study every box office hit, you will see they all feature expensive prolific music that changes the moviegoer's mood on impact. Music is added to movies to hypnotize and mesmerize people making them susceptible to brainwashing and hyper emotionalism. The actual origins of mesmerization and hypnotism started with music, long before the pendulum and swirling figures. Hypnotists admit that music is a strong tool used by them to induce trances of suggestibility. While scientists have concluded that 10-15% of adults are highly susceptible to hypnotism, with 80-85% of children under the age of 12 being highly susceptible to hypnosis. Although keep in mind those figures are just about those classified as *"highly hypnotizable"*, everyone is capable of being hypnotized, some are just more easily hypnotized than others. It is because music is such an effective tool for hypnosis that many kids shows/movies involve music and "sing-alongs". All of those sing-alongs are methods of hypnosis, and that's how "nursery rhymes" were invented; the rhymes are typically nonsense but they were used by teachers to inculcate post-hypnotic doctrines into students. If you still doubt children are hypnotized by TV, movies, games and musical programs examine the famous words of a purple dinosaur I used to watch as a child, whose song said, "*I love you, you love me. We're a happy family.*" Whenever this lyric was uttered all the kids would sing along with the purple dinosaur. Then follow it up, "*With a great big hug and a kiss from me to you!*" However you have to be majorly hypnotized to say something like that to a stranger and mean it. If any adult said that to someone's kid and their kid repeatedly enthusiastically sang along, most parents would see how that adult is brainwashing their kid to love/trust them which will eventually lead them to believe and do whatever that singer tells them to do. But when it's some fictional corporate tv show with a singer in a costume somehow that type of indoctrination is "innocent fun" and just a "silly catchy kids' song"? Devastatingly this type of indoctrination isn't exclusive to kids' sing-along songs. Adults also sing-along to songs and whether they sing along or not is irrelevant as to whether post-hypnotic beliefs are retained by the brain and soul after listening to a song. Just as kids' songs have many actions the kids perform as part of the song, such as with the "Teapot song" where kids act like a teapot, songs for adults cause them to act like the songs say to act. The teapot song makes kids act like a teapot, the gangster songs make people act like a gangster, love songs make people act like they're in love and frequently feel as such too and songs about sex and drugs lead people to be inclined towards having sex and doing drugs. Music doesn't just alter behavior though, but the minds, personalities and spiritualities are also changed by music and that's why movies and heretical worship centers include so much music. Such is a microscopic analysis of the power of music, it will change and consume your life taking control while you get lost in the rhythm of the beats. Then get beat up by Angels in Hell or the Grave for enjoying such poisonous product. NASA even spent billions sending music into space in spaceships and space capsules saying that the music made by humans can brainwash aliens to befriend us prior to first contact. So what do you think music made by humans does to human listeners? Music is powerful enough to brainwash multiple species, it has been used as a weapon of war in the past and present. Music isn't for entertaining, it's used for enslaving. Music is not art! Music is a dangerous toxic intoxicant.

In the Quran chapter 31 verse 6 contains a stern prohibition covering both idle talk and singing saying what means:

"And of the people is he who buys the amusement of speech(idle talk) to mislead from the way of Allah without knowledge

and who takes it(Islam) in ridicule. Those will have a humiliating punishment."

Ibn 'Abbas said "Idle talk" is falsehood and singing. Some Sahabah said one and some said the other, and some said it is both.

Abu Hurairah said:

The Prophet (ﷺ) said, "The bell is one of the musical instruments of Satan."

Riyad As Salihin 1691 Grade: Sahih

Abu Umamah reported:

The Messenger of Allah ﷺ said:

"Whenever a man raises his voice in musical entertainment, Allah sends two devils to sit on his shoulders, hitting his chest with their heels until he stops."

Mujam al Kabir by Tabarani 7852

Abdullah Ibn Umar reported:

Two men came from the east and delivered speeches(which amazed the people), and the Prophet (ﷺ) said, "Some eloquent speech has the influence of magic." (some people refuse to do something and then a good eloquent speaker addresses them and then they agree to do that very thing after his speech)

Sahih Bukhari 5146

Since eloquence itself can be as effective as magic spells then I ask you what type of human speech is more eloquent than musical songs? I'm not saying that every single song is a magical spell, but some of them are perhaps more powerful than magic and it's impossible for any listener to know whether a song has been produced with magic or not. For instance, there is "Soul music". Do you really think "Soul music" has no effect on the soul? They say "it comes from the soul", but what exactly are the souls of those artists' like? Likewise many artists will say their stuff "comes from the heart", well just what kind of hearts are these? If soul music comes from and effects the soul then what makes it so different that it causes an effect on the soul but the other types of music don't? There is no difference. Why is it that all the musicians that reach the highest levels of music are on drugs? It's because you can't humanely get to the highest levels of music naturally. In addition to that, artists are the most likely category of people to become addicts because the personality of an addict helps creativity, at a steep price. That's why if you study famous artists of the various art forms, you will learn how despite being great artists psychologically most were messed up and half-crazy with deep inner problems or "demons". It's just that mentally and emotionally healthy people are too normal to make great art, advanced art requires psychological abnormality sometimes to the extent of insanity. Truly you will not find a mentally healthy elite musician in all of history, do the research. Seriously not a single "great musician" has ever been sane. Musicians are basically crazy people who don't get locked up because they can function just enough to seem semi-stable and safe in society and people are addicted to the sounds they make. Whereas such psychological abnormalities and addiction increase one's risk of possession, especially when you add a drug like music to the mix.

Music is proven to cause unnatural and unhealthy sex drives. One reason why people today have less control over their lust and much more of it, is because they listen to a lot more music today than people in the past used to listen to. Music is also thought to trigger puberty, so listening to music can actually cause puberty to occur before it would normally occur. So the mental chemical hormones which music activates and reacts with cause a type of auditory orgasm, or "Braingasm" if you will. Essentially if one considers the extreme effect that pornography has on the eyes, music has a similar effect on the ears and both drastically alter and change the structure of your brain. Music actually causes brain damage and chemical imbalances. People say a picture is worth a thousand words, but a single musical note conveys a thousand pictures worth of messages to your brain and your ears can't decode or filter it, the brain absorbs it all and the musical pollution takes its toll. If you get exposed and become a music junkie you can lose your soul. If you critically analyze musical lyrics (don't listen to the music) you will see the same exact pattern and satanic messages throughout them all, even the purportedly religious ones. Even if there were religious songs, they'd be hooking people on the musical drug, but there is no such thing as a religious song; at least not one that calls to the true religion of God. I know this because I myself wrote songs that were "religious" and when re-reading the lyrics I see them as satanic now. All of my rhymes were actually crimes.

Although when I wrote them, I originally thought they were calling people to goodness and God. I wrote such lyrics without even knowing the Satanic messages they contained and had good intentions at the time. The lesson is it doesn't matter what the words of a song say, music is bad even when people try to make it good. Trust me I tried my hardest to make "religious music" that taught good things that I thought God would love. But God has forbidden music and thus it is impossible to make "good music" because it's sinful in itself just like fiction aka lying. There is no good in disobeying God. Even if you try and believe that what you are doing is good, if God or a prophet says it's not then it's not and it doesn't matter if you realize how or why it's bad, it's bad; God doesn't need to prove it in detail. At the minimum, music is addictive intoxicating fiction and is sinful and therefore forbidden in many ways.

No matter how good the theoretical morals preached in a song are, the listener will get addicted to the sound. Then when they tire of the "moral song" they'll go to some other artist for their fix being attracted to the best sound. The songs which sound the best have the worst messages, because the lyrics are so immoral that they need the most hypnotic sounds in order to compensate. None of the prophets ever used music to influence others or spread their message. If music could've been useful in spreading prophetic religion then the prophets would have used it. Yet Dawah or the propagation of the

Islamic faith is not done through fiction nor music and that applies to the "vocal only non-musical" nasheeds too. Imitating the lying storytellers of fiction and the beats of musicians whether with or without music is not a method for truth tellers spreading divine guidance. For example, the "100% vocal only tracks" beatboxing style as used by nasheed artists is sinful innovation or bida. Not only is it bida as such nasheeds and beatboxing are imitating music and hence sinful on the basis of imitating sinfulness but the "vocal only tracks" are usually Hindu or Buddhist chants or mantras. Many Asian religions have mantra chants and utterances that exactly match many of the so-called vocal-only rap or nasheed background tracks many Muslims ignorantly utilize. The permissible yet generally disliked type of nasheed poem is nowhere comparable to the modern versions which are produced with advanced computer softwares that would even make you believe it was music if it wasn't expressly labeled as "vocal-only". Furthermore, nasheeds are not meant for Islamic propaganda, it is primarily only heretics and/or foolish people who use nasheeds to teach Islam. Conclusively no prophet of God used music to preach though they had the ability to do so. Music is not limited to being only fictional but if it is used in worship or propagation of religion it then becomes a type of wicked innovative Bida.

As an author, I hope that through this book you will learn that every book and work teaches a religious message even if they don't claim or intend to do so. Thus any message that comes to you through any way messages are conveyed, fictional or otherwise, virtually or through reality, it is a type of religious propaganda. Put simply, <u>there is no such thing as a non-religious message.</u> Because even the choice of priority of information to be conveyed and the way it is conveyed involves religious lessons. Morals are a part of religion and religion cannot be removed from communication methods. So whatever it is you are doing or communicating it becomes a religious act teaching a religious message to the world. Any type of entertainment you choose to entertain yourself with is also teaching religious messages to you whether you want them to or not. Hence every joke is religious and has to do with religion, there is no such thing as a non-religious joke. Religion is an integral unavoidable part of life that plays a dominant role in everything at every moment in every person's life. Now you know. Without knowing this one is at risk of the false religions and their evil messages. As you proceed with life be aware of how religion is in everything and be aware of the fiction that something can be "unreligious" or "just for fun". Thinking everything has to do with religion, is not fanatical, it's factual. Those who think there is something that has nothing to do with religion are simply spiritually unaware and ignorant. God has decreed our entire life is a religious existence that we will be personally judged for on the Day of Resurrection. The peddlers of fiction are false prophets in disguise. While I'm not a prophet I do teach a religion just the same, it's impossible not to. I'm just letting you know that you reading anything or being a consumer of any type of message in any format is a religious activity that should help you become a better person. When reading this book your goal should be to be better after reading what I wrote. If you are reading and don't plan to be better after reading, then I strongly suggest you become a better reader who reads better with the goal of getting better as a result of reading what I've written. It can be fun to read, but this is not to be read for entertainment. This book is a form of direct communication from me to you. Consider every book or type of media/entertainment as a type of direct communication and take whatever is true and good and reject whatever is false and bad and don't even bother trying to sift through the content of those known to be corrupt; due to the delusional doctrine of taking the good and leaving the bad from every source. Taking the good and leaving the bad/mistakes only applies to known good sources. You don't act like a fool going to heretics or villains to learn from them hoping to snatch a nugget of goodness and ignoring all their evilness. Never fall in love with any author. The only books that are flawless are those of divine revelation and the only people who you can trust to be right 100% of the time are legitimate prophets of God. Any book written by anyone else will never be perfect. My book isn't perfect but it might have some good stuff in it that can help you. Books are tools, that can help or harm you, therefore read this book as God and then his prophets would want you to. My goal in writing should be to please our Creator and your goal in reading should be to please our Creator and be a better person after reading my words than you were before reading. Therefore if anything I write in this book is right and good you should read it the right way and react to it the right way. Your intentions reading/watching anything should be to please your Creator. I could try to influence you without telling you "for the greater good" but that's not how the prophets of God operated. The prophets preached to please God, that was their #1 goal. They never pretended they had no motives to influence people to think and act different/better, they all publicly admitted they wanted people to be different after hearing their religious messages of propaganda. Likewise I want you to be different/better after reading. Yet the prophets' #1 goal was NOT to convert people to their faith, they just wanted to please their Creator. When they spoke, wrote, listened, watched or read it was to please the Creator. Why do you speak, write, listen, watch or read?

Prophets are the best and most pious people whose closeness to God has been confirmed without a doubt. Prophets are more saintly than the "saints" whom people blasphemously sinfully pray to. Keep in mind that most prophets are not prayed to, nor should they be. Yet for religious shows of theater to go on they need actors to dress up and pose as a prophet. One problem with this is the impossibility of looking like someone you're not who hasn't been seen for thousands of years. No one knows what the prophets looked like since no sinful statues depicting them were ever made during their lifetimes. Secondly once we have an image of a prophet in our mind, we lose respect for them and when we think of them we will constantly think of the first image we saw that depicted them. An example would be the devil. Once people started thinking the devil had red horns, goat legs, a tail and pitchfork, the enemy of mankind became a lot less formidable because he became a symbol. Today people are even dressing up as the devil because they don't take him seriously and there are sports teams named after devils which have devils as their mascots. You might think I'm going too deep into this, but after investigation it is revealed to be an intentional plot to discredit and humiliate the prophets. The actors chosen to portray the best of mankind often don't even come close to being considered moral, even by today's immoral standards of morality. You see a guy pretending to be Moses in a play, the next time you see him he's in a movie with a beer in the right hand, a bong in the left, cocaine on his nose and a prostitute in his lap; and it gets worse. Then you read in the newsstand tabloids that he's a homosexual going through a divorce with his gay husband. The reason for the divorce being that he wants to have a sex change and become a woman thinking he's always been a woman trapped in a man's body, to which his homosexual husband disagrees. When asked whether he thinks God would approve of his transgender operation he responds that he's an atheist. Yet this is the same type of person that gets picked to portray the great prophet Moses? This will at least have a subconscious effect on the light in which the play attendees will view Moses, making it a shame that prophets have their reputation and memories smeared like this. Another example is the prophet Joseph who was put in prison for resisting attempts at being seduced by women. Joseph was the most beautiful human to have ever lived, so any actor pretending to be him is by default making him out to be uglier than he was because no make-up can match that God given beauty or even come close. Some scholars have even said that Joseph would go about with his face covered in public because his beauty was so great it led to social disruption. Therefore, any image of the prophet Joseph is automatically slander against him. Rather than pretending to be prophets, people should try to live like them. As bad as it is to have actor's dress up pretending to be prophets or to make statues of the prophets, it gets even worse. There is a Christian children's show called "Veggie Tales". The episodes revolve around animated vegetables getting into adventures which end up teaching a Christian lesson to the viewers, religious education classes frequently show episodes in class. These "Veggie tales" depict our great prophets as vegetables. The mighty King David is represented as a baby piece of asparagus! The warrior prophet Joshua is depicted as a cucumber! In another production the great prophet Jonah is shown as a piece of asparagus with a monocle! Do you know what food the prophet Joseph, the most beautiful man who lived, is portrayed as? A cucumber! These veggie tales are demeaning and derogatory to the best men who ever lived, tarnishing their reputations. Even if one attempted to justify making statues of the prophets, even though this is totally prohibited by the 2nd commandment allegedly given to Moses, there is no way someone can justify using animated vegetables to represent our beloved role models. These "Veggie Tales" even depict the famous Messenger Moses. Can you guess what they depict this great man who talked to God as? They animate Moses as a gourd! But it doesn't stop there, they also depict Abraham in one episode. Abraham who is known as the friend of God, who passed every test God ever gave him, suffers the humiliation of being portrayed as a grape. A grape! How can they turn the friend of God into a grape?! These shows are completely disrespectful, it doesn't matter what the lessons are, these animations are criminal satanic slanders and that's even if they were based on genuine scriptures which they are not. Do you think a child will respect or emulate someone who they saw depicted as a vegetable? Why do we let our prophets get insulted?

In one of the many different Christian English bibles, 2 Kings 2:23-24 narrates what happened to kids who made fun of the prophet Elisha:

"From there Elisha went up to Bethel. As he was walking along the road, some boys came out of the town and jeered at him. "Get out of here, baldy!" they said. "Get out of here, baldy!" [24] <u>*He turned around, looked at them and called down a curse on them in the name of the Lord.*</u> *Then two bears came out of the woods and mauled forty-two of the boys."*

If this is what happened to young boys according to the English translation of the New International Version of the Bible(not to be confused with the Torah given to Moses or Zabur given to David or the Injeel given to Jesus) when they taunted the prophet Elisha for being bald, then how hateful is it to God when people today slander prophets? Notice that these rude boys were not explicitly described as being disbelievers, they were just making fun of a bald guy who was missing some hair whom they might not have even known was a prophet. Yet biblically this great prophet cursed them in the name of the Lord and two bears utterly ruined them. This biblical account shows us how dangerous it can be to make fun of a prophet. Now if all these kids were mauled/killed because of their comments regarding a prophet's haircut, then what do you think God's view is regarding some bum who dresses up pretending they are a prophet for a movie, play or skit? These kids were physically annihilated simply for making comments about a prophet's haircut, imagine someone who dresses up as a prophet and has a lot more inaccuracies than just the haircut? Then what do these actors do? They put on make-up as well! Thus they are insulting the prophets automatically because they know the prophets didn't use make-up because they didn't have it or need it. Thus such people by using make-up while defaming the prophets are implying the prophets were ugly because they didn't use make-up. If that's not what they're implying they wouldn't use the make-up or the stylists, or the gels or the special lighting effects or the perfume. Yes, by putting on the perfumes they are saying the prophets stunk and they don't want to stink like they claim the prophets did. But do you know who actually started the whole trend of putting on plays with people pretending to be prophets like Jesus? It was Delmar Darrah who started this practice, and guess what? He was a freemason. It was the freemasons who began all these plays and movies about the prophets. For instance, the famous "Ten Commandments" movie was first made in 1923 CE by Cecil De Mille who was a freemason, then it was remade in 1956 CE. Again not to be conspiratorial but it was the freemasons who started this and promoted it. Many know the actor Charlton Heston who pretended to be Moses in the 1956 movie, but they don't know that Cecil De Mille also had Charlton Heston act for him 4 years earlier in his movie called "The Greatest Show on Earth". In that movie Charlton Heston was the ringleader of a circus, then 4 years later the same Director picks the same actor to be Moses. However, Charlton Heston's career didn't stop at Moses, in 1959 CE he played a fictional character in "Ben Hur" where he allegedly witnessed Jesus get crucified, in 1961 CE in "El Cid" he played a Crusader who fought in the Reconquista of Spain, while in 1954 CE Heston played a tomb raider who recovered a "sunburst" pagan Incan idol and kindly gave it to the Incans so they could worship their "sunburst" idol in its temple. So 4 years before he acted as Moses this guy acted as a circus ring-leader, and 2 years before he acted as Moses he acted as someone helping pagans worship a "sunburst" idol. While the freemason film director Cecil de Mille also made immoral films like, "*The Woman God Forgot*", "*The Devil Stone*", "*Old Wives for New*", "*Forbidden Fruit*", "*Adam's Rib*", "*The Crusaders*", "*Fool's Paradise*", "*The Godless Girl*", "*Madame Satan*", "*Cleopatra*" and several slanderous films about Jesus which I won't even mention because they are so bad. The very guy who popularized movies about the prophets was a clear enemy to these same prophets. So how can people today say movies about prophets of God are okay when the whole prophetic movie genre was made by bad guys who hated and blasphemed these prophets? It is a fact that the movies about prophets were made to insult them. It's cause and effect, because of these religious movies about prophets many people stopped loving the prophets or trying to believe in and practice their prophetic religion. Far from being the cure, these allegedly religious movies about prophets contributed to the anti-religious disease. One of the worst things one can do to harm the image of a prophet is to make a movie or picture depicting them. These filthy movie producers have become the new prophets of the masses and their movies are treated as if they were divine revelations. The world's various faiths have been replaced with films. Instead of Scripture, now people prefer a movie script. People are selling their tickets to paradise for movie tickets and ticking off God in the process.

Also the kids who got attacked by bears because of their attitude amounting to an attack on the prophet, were just criticizing the prophet for an actual physical trait, they weren't lying about him saying something about him that was false. Today many people call prophets and messengers of God drunkards, incestuous, liars, magicians, possessed, ignorant, foolish, adulterous, pedophiles and all other kinds of filthy derogatory things which are completely false and untrue regarding the many prophets who are incorrectly given such labels. Considering what the various bibles say happened to people jeering at the physical appearance of a prophet, then by default any depiction of a prophet would also be a form of slander that would put one in the same category as these boys who were mauled by bears. By depicting a prophet inaccurately, it could make one cursed by God. Yet today not only are the prophets depicted and slandered, but they are depicted as pieces of food! We wouldn't think it was respectful to depict the president, king or leader of a country as food so then why do we let our spiritual leaders and messengers sent to us by God suffer such degradation? Do we love our politicians more than our prophets? Do we know more about politicians than we do the prophets? Do we obey politicians more than our prophets? Do we support politicians more than our prophets? If you went to paradise and met the prophets what would you say if they asked you what did you do or how did you feel when they were getting slandered and depicted in such humiliating and disgraceful ways? What will we say to God when he asks us about our attitudes towards the prophets? We are supposed to love God's prophets more than we do ourselves. If we really loved the magnificent prophets and messengers God sent to us then we would strongly dislike all these depictions which get made of them and the mockeries people make about them in movies, plays and other theatrical performances. Even that such disgusting depictions are portrayed as "performances" are offensive. The prophets were not performers. What they did was believe what God wanted them to believe, live how God wanted them to live and do what God wanted them to do. Protesting like disbelieving hooligans was not part of the prophetic methodology. So don't protest these false portrayals either. Instead actually study the prophetic faith and apply it in your daily life until death. For the prophets it wasn't an act or a show, it was real life. You don't copy that and "re-enact the prophets", we're supposed to be living it practicing the same religion that they did daily. You live it, you don't watch it. The prophets didn't put on such performances depicting previous prophets because they were too busy actually living how God wanted them to live and doing good deeds. Jesus never dressed up as Moses to put on a show and motivate people. David never dressed up as Abraham. Moses never dressed up as Noah. Muhammad never dressed up as Solomon. The theatrical arts came from Greece and there were only two types of plays or performances. There were tragedies and comedies. No prophet's life was a tragedy and no prophet's life was a comedy. So it is impossible for there to ever be a performance depicting the prophets' lives. If it was possible and beneficial the prophets would have done it themselves, because the very reason they were created was to motivate people to worship God and follow the prophetic examples. But what's more is how all the prophets taught people to give in charity. Guess what? These movies, tv shows, plays, comics, songs, nasheeds, skits, and the other nonsense people make depicting prophets are not free. They cost money, so instead of people giving in charity like the prophets said to, instead people waste their wealth to create, watch or see/hear something about people who taught our species that we should give in charity. Thereby in creating and consuming such material people are contradicting the very prophets such filthy material claims to be about. Then what do they do? Do they give in charity every day for the rest of their life after watching the prophetic performance? Nope! Most of them don't even give charity at all let alone out of direct motivation from the allegedly motivational performances. What do they do instead? They stand up and give a round of applause with everyone clapping and crying and glorifying these fraudulent imposters and literal "false-prophets" profiteering racket. Seriously they don't boo, heckle or ridicule or even criticize, they congratulate, support and encourage this antagonistic carnage. They literally do the exact opposite of what good people would do. If we see this junk, we shouldn't consume it at all nor promote it. If we do anything we should denounce such "false-prophets" and filthy depictions. It is simply an entertainment business, movies and plays are made for money and not many people will pay money to see the truth, it is much easier to sell a lie. Besides all actors and actresses are sinfully bearing false witness by acting anyways so they are lying even if it's not a purely fictional script. Most of the Ahl-Kitab (people of Scripture) today are Ahl-TV (people of Television) and they spend more time watching a screen of sinfulness than studying the faith they profess. Hence people become heartless due to mindless heart numbing entertainment that creates a cycle of depression and desensitization to sin. Many people today spend more time in the realm of fiction than they do in reality. We really must stop supporting such sinful fictional activities in all formats and detox devoting ourself to the true divinity and read God's final revelation the Quran and authentic prophetic teachings of Muhammad via the Hadith acting upon them with sincerity. As an admonition and reminder, the rest of this book will consist of some evidence from the

Quran and Hadith that prohibit lying which is well known as sinful and covers all genres of every type of fiction which is just as sinful as lying though often mistakenly indulged in by the forgetful. Try to remember when you forget the remembrance of Allah you forget the enemies of Allah and their plots. Also remember that every sin decreases your faith just as every sincere good deed done according to the prophetic faith increases it. Fiction spreading throughout the world simultaneously weakens the popularity of the truth and toxifies the real world further due to the epidemic of falsehood being normalized as entertainment and otherwise. While I have focused primarily on fiction as being forbidden, lying as a type of non-entertainment is no less dangerous or damnable. Fiction is forbidden because it requires lying and lying is forbidden by Allah for a plethora of reasons as shall be shown. Don't mistake fiction as being other than a lie and don't underestimate the danger of non-artistic lies either. I just focused on fiction, enshrined in many countries under the guise of freedom, because it is often undetected as falsehood and mistakenly imagined to be the same as creativity. As far as media goes you are likely more exposed to fiction than you are to non-artistic lies. Nevertheless, all lies lead to the blaze of hellfire and the people of truth have nothing to do with lies or liars whether they are famous popular forms of entertainment or otherwise. For all fiction leads to failure in this life as well as the eternal afterlife. God blesses those few who resist the sins of lying and fiction of all formats.

QURAN AYAT FORBIDDING LIES

Quran 2:8-10

وَمِنَ ٱلنَّاسِ مَن يَقُولُ ءَامَنَّا بِٱللَّهِ وَبِٱلْيَوْمِ ٱلْأَخِرِ وَمَا هُم
بِمُؤْمِنِينَ (٨) يُخَـٰدِعُونَ ٱللَّهَ وَٱلَّذِينَ ءَامَنُوا۟ وَمَا يَخْدَعُونَ إِلَّا
أَنفُسَهُمْ وَمَا يَشْعُرُونَ (٩) فِى قُلُوبِهِم مَّرَضٌ فَزَادَهُمُ ٱللَّهُ
مَرَضًا ۖ وَلَهُمْ عَذَابٌ أَلِيمٌ بِمَا كَانُوا۟ يَكْذِبُونَ (١٠)

And of the people are some who say, "We believe in Allah and the Last Day," but they are not believers. (8) They [think to] deceive Allah and those who believe, but they deceive not except themselves and perceive [it] not. (9) In their hearts is disease, so Allah has increased their disease; and for them is a painful punishment because they [habitually] used to lie. (10)

Quran 2:79-80

فَوَيْلٌ لِّلَّذِينَ يَكْتُبُونَ ٱلْكِتَـٰبَ بِأَيْدِيهِمْ ثُمَّ يَقُولُونَ هَـٰذَا مِنْ عِندِ ٱللَّهِ لِيَشْتَرُوا۟ بِهِۦ ثَمَنًا قَلِيلًۭا ۖ فَوَيْلٌۭ لَّهُم مِّمَّا كَتَبَتْ أَيْدِيهِمْ وَوَيْلٌۭ لَّهُم مِّمَّا يَكْسِبُونَ (٧٩) وَقَالُوا۟ لَن تَمَسَّنَا ٱلنَّارُ إِلَّآ أَيَّامًۭا مَّعْدُودَةًۭ ۚ قُلْ أَتَّخَذْتُمْ عِندَ ٱللَّهِ عَهْدًۭا فَلَن يُخْلِفَ ٱللَّهُ عَهْدَهُۥٓ ۖ أَمْ تَقُولُونَ عَلَى ٱللَّهِ مَا لَا تَعْلَمُونَ (٨٠)

So woe to those who write the "scripture" with their own hands, then say, "This is from Allah," in order to exchange it for a small price. Woe to them for what their hands have written and woe to them for what they earn. (79) And they say, "Never will the Fire touch us, except for a few days." Say, "Have you taken a covenant with Allah? For Allah will never break His covenant. Or do you say about Allah that which you do not know?" (80)

Quran 2:140

أَمْ تَقُولُونَ إِنَّ إِبْرَٰهِـۧمَ وَإِسْمَـٰعِيلَ وَإِسْحَـٰقَ وَيَعْقُوبَ وَٱلْأَسْبَاطَ كَانُوا۟ هُودًا أَوْ نَصَـٰرَىٰ ۗ قُلْ ءَأَنتُمْ أَعْلَمُ أَمِ ٱللَّهُ ۗ وَمَنْ أَظْلَمُ مِمَّن كَتَمَ شَهَـٰدَةً عِندَهُۥ مِنَ ٱللَّهِ ۗ وَمَا ٱللَّهُ بِغَـٰفِلٍ عَمَّا تَعْمَلُونَ (١٤٠)

Or do you say that Abraham and Ishmael and Isaac and Jacob and the Descendants were Jews or Christians? Say, "Are you more knowing or is Allah?" And who is more unjust than one who conceals a testimony he has from Allah? And Allah is not unaware of what you do. (140)

Quran 2:146

ٱلَّذِينَ ءَاتَيْنَٰهُمُ ٱلْكِتَٰبَ يَعْرِفُونَهُۥ كَمَا يَعْرِفُونَ أَبْنَآءَهُمْ ۖ وَإِنَّ فَرِيقًا مِّنْهُمْ لَيَكْتُمُونَ ٱلْحَقَّ وَهُمْ يَعْلَمُونَ (١٤٦)

Those to whom We gave the Scripture know him as they know their own sons. But indeed, a party of them conceal the truth while they know [it]. (146)

Quran 2:159-162

إِنَّ ٱلَّذِينَ يَكْتُمُونَ مَآ أَنزَلْنَا مِنَ ٱلْبَيِّنَٰتِ وَٱلْهُدَىٰ مِنۢ بَعْدِ مَا بَيَّنَّٰهُ لِلنَّاسِ فِى ٱلْكِتَٰبِ أُو۟لَٰٓئِكَ يَلْعَنُهُمُ ٱللَّهُ وَيَلْعَنُهُمُ ٱللَّٰعِنُونَ (١٥٩) إِلَّا ٱلَّذِينَ تَابُوا۟ وَأَصْلَحُوا۟ وَبَيَّنُوا۟ فَأُو۟لَٰٓئِكَ أَتُوبُ عَلَيْهِمْ ۚ وَأَنَا ٱلتَّوَّابُ ٱلرَّحِيمُ (١٦٠) إِنَّ ٱلَّذِينَ كَفَرُوا۟ وَمَاتُوا۟ وَهُمْ كُفَّارٌ أُو۟لَٰٓئِكَ عَلَيْهِمْ لَعْنَةُ ٱللَّهِ وَٱلْمَلَٰٓئِكَةِ وَٱلنَّاسِ أَجْمَعِينَ

(١٦١) خَٰلِدِينَ فِيهَا لَا يُخَفَّفُ عَنْهُمُ ٱلْعَذَابُ وَلَا هُمْ يُنظَرُونَ (١٦٢)

Indeed, those who conceal what We sent down of clear proofs and guidance after We made it clear for the people in the Scripture - those are cursed by Allah and cursed by those who curse, (159) Except for those who repent and correct themselves and make evident [what they concealed]. Those - I will accept their repentance, and I am the Accepting of repentance, the Merciful. (160) Indeed, those who disbelieve and die while they are disbelievers - upon them will be the curse of Allah and of the angels and the people, all together, (161) Abiding eternally therein. The punishment will not be lightened for them, nor will they be reprieved. (162)

Quran 2:174-175

إِنَّ ٱلَّذِينَ يَكْتُمُونَ مَآ أَنزَلَ ٱللَّهُ مِنَ ٱلْكِتَٰبِ وَيَشْتَرُونَ بِهِۦ ثَمَنًا قَلِيلًا أُو۟لَٰٓئِكَ مَا يَأْكُلُونَ فِى بُطُونِهِمْ إِلَّا ٱلنَّارَ وَلَا يُكَلِّمُهُمُ ٱللَّهُ يَوْمَ ٱلْقِيَٰمَةِ وَلَا يُزَكِّيهِمْ وَلَهُمْ عَذَابٌ أَلِيمٌ (١٧٤) أُو۟لَٰٓئِكَ ٱلَّذِينَ ٱشْتَرَوُا۟ ٱلضَّلَٰلَةَ بِٱلْهُدَىٰ وَٱلْعَذَابَ بِٱلْمَغْفِرَةِ فَمَآ أَصْبَرَهُمْ عَلَى ٱلنَّارِ (١٧٥)

Indeed, they who conceal what Allah has sent down of the Book and exchange it for a small price - those consume not into their bellies except the Fire. And Allah will not speak to them on the Day of Resurrection, nor will He purify them. And they will have a painful punishment. (174) Those are the ones who have exchanged guidance for error and forgiveness for punishment. How patient they are in pursuit of the Fire! (175)

Quran 2:228

وَٱلْمُطَلَّقَٰتُ يَتَرَبَّصْنَ بِأَنفُسِهِنَّ ثَلَٰثَةَ قُرُوٓءٍ وَلَا يَحِلُّ لَهُنَّ أَن يَكْتُمْنَ مَا خَلَقَ ٱللَّهُ فِىٓ أَرْحَامِهِنَّ إِن كُنَّ يُؤْمِنَّ بِٱللَّهِ وَٱلْيَوْمِ ٱلْءَاخِرِ وَبُعُولَتُهُنَّ أَحَقُّ بِرَدِّهِنَّ فِى ذَٰلِكَ إِنْ أَرَادُوٓا۟ إِصْلَٰحًا وَلَهُنَّ مِثْلُ ٱلَّذِى عَلَيْهِنَّ بِٱلْمَعْرُوفِ وَلِلرِّجَالِ عَلَيْهِنَّ دَرَجَةٌ وَٱللَّهُ عَزِيزٌ حَكِيمٌ (٢٢٨)

Divorced women remain in waiting for three periods, and it is not lawful for them to conceal what Allah has created in their wombs if they believe in Allah and the Last Day. And their husbands have more right to take them back in this [period] if they want reconciliation. And due to the wives is similar to what is expected of them, according to what is reasonable. But the men have a degree over them [in responsibility and authority]. And Allah is Exalted in Might and Wise. (228)

Quran 2:283-284

۞ وَإِن كُنتُمْ عَلَىٰ سَفَرٍ وَلَمْ تَجِدُوا۟ كَاتِبًا فَرِهَٰنٌ مَّقْبُوضَةٌ ۖ فَإِنْ أَمِنَ بَعْضُكُم بَعْضًا فَلْيُؤَدِّ ٱلَّذِى ٱؤْتُمِنَ أَمَٰنَتَهُۥ وَلْيَتَّقِ ٱللَّهَ رَبَّهُۥ ۗ وَلَا تَكْتُمُوا۟ ٱلشَّهَٰدَةَ ۚ وَمَن يَكْتُمْهَا فَإِنَّهُۥٓ ءَاثِمٌ قَلْبُهُۥ ۗ وَٱللَّهُ بِمَا تَعْمَلُونَ عَلِيمٌ (٢٨٣) لِّلَّهِ مَا فِى ٱلسَّمَٰوَٰتِ وَمَا فِى ٱلْأَرْضِ ۗ وَإِن تُبْدُوا۟ مَا فِىٓ أَنفُسِكُمْ أَوْ تُخْفُوهُ يُحَاسِبْكُم بِهِ ٱللَّهُ ۖ فَيَغْفِرُ لِمَن يَشَآءُ وَيُعَذِّبُ مَن يَشَآءُ ۗ وَٱللَّهُ عَلَىٰ كُلِّ شَىْءٍ قَدِيرٌ (٢٨٤)

And if you are on a journey and cannot find a scribe, then a security deposit [should be] taken. And if one of you entrusts another, then let him who is entrusted discharge his trust [faithfully] and let him fear Allah, his Lord. And do not conceal testimony, for whoever conceals it - his heart is indeed sinful, and Allah is Knowing of what you do. (283) To Allah belongs whatever is in the heavens and whatever is in the earth. Whether you show what is within yourselves or conceal it, Allah will bring you to account for it. Then He will forgive whom He wills and punish whom He wills, and Allah is over all things competent. (284)

Quran 3:71

يَـٰٓأَهۡلَ ٱلۡكِتَـٰبِ لِمَ تَلۡبِسُونَ ٱلۡحَقَّ بِٱلۡبَـٰطِلِ وَتَكۡتُمُونَ ٱلۡحَقَّ وَأَنتُمۡ تَعۡلَمُونَ (٧١)

O People of the Scripture, why do you confuse the truth with falsehood and conceal the truth while you know [it]? (71)

Quran 3:75

۞ وَمِنْ أَهْلِ ٱلْكِتَـٰبِ مَنْ إِن تَأْمَنْهُ بِقِنطَارٍ يُؤَدِّهِۦ إِلَيْكَ وَمِنْهُم مَّنْ إِن تَأْمَنْهُ بِدِينَارٍ لَّا يُؤَدِّهِۦ إِلَيْكَ إِلَّا مَا دُمْتَ عَلَيْهِ قَآئِمًا ذَٰلِكَ بِأَنَّهُمْ قَالُوا۟ لَيْسَ عَلَيْنَا فِى ٱلْأُمِّيِّـۧنَ سَبِيلٌ وَيَقُولُونَ عَلَى ٱللَّهِ ٱلْكَذِبَ وَهُمْ يَعْلَمُونَ (٧٥)

And among the People of the Scripture is he who, if you entrust him with a great amount [of wealth], he will return it to you. And among them is he who, if you entrust him with a [single] silver coin, he will not return it to you unless you are constantly standing over him [demanding it]. That is because they say, "There is no blame upon us concerning the unlearned." And they speak untruth about Allah while they know [it]. (75)

Quran 3:77-78

إِنَّ ٱلَّذِينَ يَشْتَرُونَ بِعَهْدِ ٱللَّهِ وَأَيْمَٰنِهِمْ ثَمَنًا قَلِيلاً أُوْلَٰئِكَ لَا خَلَٰقَ لَهُمْ فِى ٱلْأَخِرَةِ وَلَا يُكَلِّمُهُمُ ٱللَّهُ وَلَا يَنظُرُ إِلَيْهِمْ يَوْمَ ٱلْقِيَٰمَةِ وَلَا يُزَكِّيهِمْ وَلَهُمْ عَذَابٌ أَلِيمٌ (٧٧) وَإِنَّ مِنْهُمْ لَفَرِيقًا يَلْوُ ۥنَ أَلْسِنَتَهُم بِٱلْكِتَٰبِ لِتَحْسَبُوهُ مِنَ ٱلْكِتَٰبِ وَمَا هُوَ مِنَ ٱلْكِتَٰبِ وَيَقُولُونَ هُوَ مِنْ عِندِ ٱللَّهِ وَمَا هُوَ مِنْ عِندِ ٱللَّهِ وَيَقُولُونَ عَلَى ٱللَّهِ ٱلْكَذِبَ وَهُمْ يَعْلَمُونَ (٧٨)

Indeed, those who exchange the covenant of Allah and their [own] oaths for a small price will have no share in the Hereafter, and Allah will not speak to them or look at them on the Day of Resurrection, nor will He purify them; and they will have a painful punishment. (77) And indeed, there is among them a party who alter the Scripture with their tongues so you may think it is from the Scripture, but it is not from the Scripture. And they say, "This is from Allah," but it is not from Allah. And they speak untruth about Allah while they know. (78)

Quran 3:93-95

۞ كُلُّ ٱلطَّعَامِ كَانَ حِلًّا لِّبَنِىٓ إِسْرَٰٓءِيلَ إِلَّا مَا حَرَّمَ إِسْرَٰٓءِيلُ عَلَىٰ نَفْسِهِۦ مِن قَبْلِ أَن تُنَزَّلَ ٱلتَّوْرَىٰةُ قُلْ فَأْتُوا۟ بِٱلتَّوْرَىٰةِ فَٱتْلُوهَآ إِن كُنتُمْ صَٰدِقِينَ (٩٣) فَمَنِ ٱفْتَرَىٰ عَلَى ٱللَّهِ ٱلْكَذِبَ مِنۢ بَعْدِ ذَٰلِكَ فَأُو۟لَٰٓئِكَ هُمُ ٱلظَّٰلِمُونَ (٩٤) قُلْ صَدَقَ ٱللَّهُ فَٱتَّبِعُوا۟ مِلَّةَ إِبْرَٰهِيمَ حَنِيفًا وَمَا كَانَ مِنَ ٱلْمُشْرِكِينَ (٩٥)

All food was lawful to the Children of Israel except what Israel had made unlawful to himself before the Torah was revealed. Say, [O Muhammad], "So bring the Torah and recite it, if you should be truthful."
(93) And whoever invents about Allah untruth after that - then those are [truly] the wrongdoers. (94) Say, "Allah has told the truth. So follow the religion of Abraham, inclining toward truth; and he was not of the polytheists." (95)

Quran 4:107-108

وَلَا تُجَٰدِلْ عَنِ ٱلَّذِينَ يَخْتَانُونَ أَنفُسَهُمْ إِنَّ ٱللَّهَ لَا يُحِبُّ مَن كَانَ خَوَّانًا أَثِيمًا (١٠٧) يَسْتَخْفُونَ مِنَ ٱلنَّاسِ وَلَا يَسْتَخْفُونَ

مِنَ ٱللَّهِ وَهُوَ مَعَهُمْ إِذْ يُبَيِّتُونَ مَا لَا يَرْضَىٰ مِنَ ٱلْقَوْلِ وَكَانَ ٱللَّهُ بِمَا يَعْمَلُونَ مُحِيطًا (١٠٨)

And do not argue on behalf of those who deceive themselves. Indeed, Allah loves not one who is a habitually sinful deceiver. (107) They conceal [their evil intentions and deeds] from the people, but they cannot conceal [them] from Allah, and He is with them [in His knowledge] when they spend the night in such as He does not accept of speech. And ever is Allah, of what they do, encompassing. (108)

Quran 4:112

وَمَن يَكْسِبْ خَطِيئَةً أَوْ إِثْمًا ثُمَّ يَرْمِ بِهِۦ بَرِيًّا فَقَدِ ٱحْتَمَلَ بُهْتَٰنًا وَإِثْمًا مُّبِينًا (١١٢)

But whoever earns an offense or a sin and then blames it on an innocent [person] has taken upon himself a slander and manifest sin. (112)

Quran 4:156-158

وَبِكُفْرِهِمْ وَقَوْلِهِمْ عَلَىٰ مَرْيَمَ بُهْتَـٰنًا عَظِيمًا (١٥٦) وَقَوْلِهِمْ
إِنَّا قَتَلْنَا ٱلْمَسِيحَ عِيسَى ٱبْنَ مَرْيَمَ رَسُولَ ٱللَّهِ وَمَا قَتَلُوهُ وَمَا
صَلَبُوهُ وَلَـٰكِن شُبِّهَ لَهُمْ وَإِنَّ ٱلَّذِينَ ٱخْتَلَفُوا فِيهِ لَفِى شَكٍّ مِّنْهُ
مَا لَهُم بِهِۦ مِنْ عِلْمٍ إِلَّا ٱتِّبَاعَ ٱلظَّنِّ وَمَا قَتَلُوهُ يَقِينًا
(١٥٧) بَل رَّفَعَهُ ٱللَّهُ إِلَيْهِ وَكَانَ ٱللَّهُ عَزِيزًا حَكِيمًا (١٥٨)

And [We cursed them] for their disbelief and their saying against Mary a great slander, (156) And [for] their saying, "Indeed, we have killed the Messiah, Jesus, the son of Mary, the messenger of Allah." And they did not kill him, nor did they crucify him; but [another] was made to resemble him to them. And indeed, those who differ over it are in doubt about it. They have no knowledge of it except the following of assumption. And they did not kill him, for certain. (157) Rather, Allah raised him to Himself. And ever is Allah Exalted in Might and Wise. (158)

Quran 5:41-42

146

۞ يَـٰٓأَيُّهَا ٱلرَّسُولُ لَا يَحْزُنكَ ٱلَّذِينَ يُسَـٰرِعُونَ فِى ٱلْكُفْرِ مِنَ ٱلَّذِينَ قَالُوٓاْ ءَامَنَّا بِأَفْوَٰهِهِمْ وَلَمْ تُؤْمِن قُلُوبُهُمْ وَمِنَ ٱلَّذِينَ هَادُواْ سَمَّـٰعُونَ لِلْكَذِبِ سَمَّـٰعُونَ لِقَوْمٍ ءَاخَرِينَ لَمْ يَأْتُوكَ يُحَرِّفُونَ ٱلْكَلِمَ مِنۢ بَعْدِ مَوَاضِعِهِ يَقُولُونَ إِنْ أُوتِيتُمْ هَـٰذَا فَخُذُوهُ وَإِن لَّمْ تُؤْتَوْهُ فَٱحْذَرُواْ وَمَن يُرِدِ ٱللَّهُ فِتْنَتَهُ فَلَن تَمْلِكَ لَهُۥ مِنَ ٱللَّهِ شَيْـًٔا أُوْلَـٰٓئِكَ ٱلَّذِينَ لَمْ يُرِدِ ٱللَّهُ أَن يُطَهِّرَ قُلُوبَهُمْ لَهُمْ فِى ٱلدُّنْيَا خِزْىٌ وَلَهُمْ فِى ٱلْـَٔاخِرَةِ عَذَابٌ عَظِيمٌ (٤١) سَمَّـٰعُونَ لِلْكَذِبِ أَكَّـٰلُونَ لِلسُّحْتِ فَإِن جَآءُوكَ فَٱحْكُم بَيْنَهُمْ أَوْ أَعْرِضْ عَنْهُمْ وَإِن تُعْرِضْ عَنْهُمْ فَلَن يَضُرُّوكَ شَيْـًٔا وَإِنْ حَكَمْتَ فَٱحْكُم بَيْنَهُم بِٱلْقِسْطِ إِنَّ ٱللَّهَ يُحِبُّ ٱلْمُقْسِطِينَ (٤٢)

O Messenger, let them not grieve you who hasten into disbelief of those who say, "We believe" with their mouths, but their hearts believe not, and from among the Jews. [They are] avid listeners to falsehood, listening to another people who have not come to you. They distort words beyond their [proper] usages, saying "If you are given this, take it; but if you are not given it, then beware." But he for whom Allah intends fitnah - never will you possess [power to do] for him *a thing against Allah. Those are the ones for whom Allah does not intend to purify their hearts. For them in this world is disgrace, and for them in the Hereafter is a great punishment. (41) [They are] avid listeners to falsehood, devourers of [what is] unlawful. So if they come to you, [O Muhammad], judge between them or turn away from them. And if you turn away from them - never will they harm you at all. And if you judge, judge between them with justice. Indeed, Allah loves those who act justly. (42)*

Quran 5:61-63

وَإِذَا جَآءُوكُمْ قَالُوٓا۟ ءَامَنَّا وَقَد دَّخَلُوا۟ بِٱلْكُفْرِ وَهُمْ قَدْ خَرَجُوا۟ بِهِۦ ۚ وَٱللَّهُ أَعْلَمُ بِمَا كَانُوا۟ يَكْتُمُونَ (٦١) وَتَرَىٰ كَثِيرًا مِّنْهُمْ يُسَٰرِعُونَ فِى ٱلْإِثْمِ وَٱلْعُدْوَٰنِ وَأَكْلِهِمُ ٱلسُّحْتَ ۚ لَبِئْسَ مَا كَانُوا۟ يَعْمَلُونَ (٦٢) لَوْلَا يَنْهَٰهُمُ ٱلرَّبَّٰنِيُّونَ وَٱلْأَحْبَارُ عَن قَوْلِهِمُ ٱلْإِثْمَ وَأَكْلِهِمُ ٱلسُّحْتَ ۚ لَبِئْسَ مَا كَانُوا۟ يَصْنَعُونَ (٦٣)

And when they come to you, they say, "We believe." But they have entered with disbelief [in their hearts], and they have certainly left with it. And Allah is most knowing of what they were concealing. (61) And you see many of them hastening into sin and aggression and the devouring of [what is] unlawful. How wretched is what they have been doing. (62) Why do the rabbis and religious scholars not forbid them from saying what is sinful and devouring what is unlawful? How wretched is what they have been practicing. (63)

Quran 5:106-108

يَٰٓأَيُّهَا ٱلَّذِينَ ءَامَنُوا۟ شَهَٰدَةُ بَيْنِكُمْ إِذَا حَضَرَ أَحَدَكُمُ ٱلْمَوْتُ حِينَ ٱلْوَصِيَّةِ ٱثْنَانِ ذَوَا عَدْلٍ مِّنكُمْ أَوْ ءَاخَرَانِ مِنْ غَيْرِكُمْ إِنْ أَنتُمْ ضَرَبْتُمْ فِى ٱلْأَرْضِ فَأَصَٰبَتْكُم مُّصِيبَةُ ٱلْمَوْتِ تَحْبِسُونَهُمَا مِنۢ بَعْدِ ٱلصَّلَوٰةِ فَيُقْسِمَانِ بِٱللَّهِ إِنِ ٱرْتَبْتُمْ لَا نَشْتَرِى بِهِۦ ثَمَنًا وَلَوْ كَانَ ذَا قُرْبَىٰ وَلَا نَكْتُمُ شَهَٰدَةَ ٱللَّهِ إِنَّآ إِذًا لَّمِنَ ٱلْءَاثِمِينَ (١٠٦) فَإِنْ عُثِرَ عَلَىٰٓ أَنَّهُمَا ٱسْتَحَقَّآ إِثْمًا فَـَٔاخَرَانِ يَقُومَانِ مَقَامَهُمَا مِنَ ٱلَّذِينَ ٱسْتَحَقَّ عَلَيْهِمُ ٱلْأَوْلَيَٰنِ فَيُقْسِمَانِ بِٱللَّهِ لَشَهَٰدَتُنَآ أَحَقُّ مِن شَهَٰدَتِهِمَا وَمَا ٱعْتَدَيْنَآ إِنَّآ إِذًا لَّمِنَ ٱلظَّٰلِمِينَ (١٠٧) ذَٰلِكَ أَدْنَىٰٓ أَن يَأْتُوا۟ بِٱلشَّهَٰدَةِ عَلَىٰٓ

وَجْهِهَا أَوْ يَخَافُوٓا۟ أَن تُرَدَّ أَيْمَـٰنٌۢ بَعْدَ أَيْمَـٰنِهِمْۗ وَٱتَّقُوا۟ ٱللَّهَ وَٱسْمَعُوا۟ۗ وَٱللَّهُ لَا يَهْدِى ٱلْقَوْمَ ٱلْفَـٰسِقِينَ (١٠٨)

O you who have believed, testimony [should be taken] among you when death approaches one of you at the time of bequest - [that of] two just men from among you or two others from outside if you are traveling through the land and the disaster of death should strike you. Detain them after the prayer and let them both swear by Allah if you doubt [their testimony, saying], "We will not exchange our oath for a price, even if he should be a near relative, and we will not withhold the testimony of Allah. Indeed, we would then be of the sinful." (106) But if it is found that those two were guilty of perjury, let two others stand in their place [who are] foremost [in claim] from those who have a lawful right. And let them swear by Allah, "Our testimony is truer than their testimony, and we have not transgressed.

Indeed, we would then be of the wrongdoers." (107) That is more likely that they will give testimony according to its [true] objective, or [at least] they would fear that [other] oaths might be taken after their oaths. And fear Allah and listen; and Allah does not guide the defiantly disobedient people. (108)

Quran 6:21-24

وَمَنْ أَظْلَمُ مِمَّنِ ٱفْتَرَىٰ عَلَى ٱللَّهِ كَذِبًا أَوْ كَذَّبَ بِـَٔايَـٰتِهِۦٓ ۗ إِنَّهُۥ لَا يُفْلِحُ ٱلظَّـٰلِمُونَ (٢١) وَيَوْمَ نَحْشُرُهُمْ جَمِيعًا ثُمَّ نَقُولُ لِلَّذِينَ أَشْرَكُوٓاْ أَيْنَ شُرَكَآؤُكُمُ ٱلَّذِينَ كُنتُمْ تَزْعُمُونَ (٢٢) ثُمَّ لَمْ تَكُن فِتْنَتُهُمْ إِلَّآ أَن قَالُواْ وَٱللَّهِ رَبِّنَا مَا كُنَّا مُشْرِكِينَ (٢٣) ٱنظُرْ كَيْفَ كَذَبُواْ عَلَىٰٓ أَنفُسِهِمْ ۚ وَضَلَّ عَنْهُم مَّا كَانُواْ يَفْتَرُونَ (٢٤)

And who is more unjust than one who invents about Allah a lie or denies His verses? Indeed, the wrongdoers will not succeed. (21) And [mention O Muhammad], the Day We will gather them all together; then We will say to those who associated

others with Allah, "Where are your
'partners' that you used to claim [with
Him]?" (22) Then there will be no [excuse
upon] examination except they will say, "By
Allah, our Lord, we were not those who
associated." (23) See how they will lie about
themselves. And lost from them will be what
they used to invent. (24)

Quran 6:27-31

وَلَوْ تَرَىٰ إِذْ وُقِفُواْ عَلَى ٱلنَّارِ فَقَالُواْ يَـٰلَيْتَنَا نُرَدُّ وَلَا نُكَذِّبَ
بِـَٔايَـٰتِ رَبِّنَا وَنَكُونَ مِنَ ٱلْمُؤْمِنِينَ (٢٧) بَلْ بَدَا لَهُم مَّا كَانُواْ
يُخْفُونَ مِن قَبْلُ وَلَوْ رُدُّواْ لَعَادُواْ لِمَا نُهُواْ عَنْهُ وَإِنَّهُمْ
لَكَـٰذِبُونَ (٢٨) وَقَالُوٓاْ إِنْ هِىَ إِلَّا حَيَاتُنَا ٱلدُّنْيَا وَمَا نَحْنُ
بِمَبْعُوثِينَ (٢٩) وَلَوْ تَرَىٰ إِذْ وُقِفُواْ عَلَىٰ رَبِّهِمْ قَالَ أَلَيْسَ
هَـٰذَا بِٱلْحَقِّ قَالُواْ بَلَىٰ وَرَبِّنَا قَالَ فَذُوقُواْ ٱلْعَذَابَ بِمَا كُنتُمْ
تَكْفُرُونَ (٣٠) قَدْ خَسِرَ ٱلَّذِينَ كَذَّبُواْ بِلِقَآءِ ٱللَّهِ حَتَّىٰٓ إِذَا
جَآءَتْهُمُ ٱلسَّاعَةُ بَغْتَةً قَالُواْ يَـٰحَسْرَتَنَا عَلَىٰ مَا فَرَّطْنَا فِيهَا
وَهُمْ يَحْمِلُونَ أَوْزَارَهُمْ عَلَىٰ ظُهُورِهِمْ أَلَا سَآءَ مَا يَزِرُونَ
(٣١)

If you could but see when they are made to
stand before the Fire and will say, "Oh,

would that we could be returned [to life on earth] and not deny the signs of our Lord and be among the believers." (27) But what they concealed before has [now] appeared to them. And even if they were returned, they would return to that which they were forbidden; and indeed, they are liars. (28) And they say, "There is none but our worldly life, and we will not be resurrected." (29) If you could but see when they will be made to stand before their Lord. He will say, "Is this not the truth?" They will say, "Yes, by our Lord." He will [then] say, "So taste the punishment because you used to disbelieve." (30) Those will have lost who deny the meeting with Allah, until when the Hour [of resurrection] comes upon them unexpectedly, they will say, "Oh, [how great is] our regret over what we neglected concerning it," while they bear their burdens on their backs. Unquestionably, evil is that which they bear. (31)

Quran 6:93-94

وَمَنْ أَظْلَمُ مِمَّنِ ٱفْتَرَىٰ عَلَى ٱللَّهِ كَذِبًا أَوْ قَالَ أُوحِىَ إِلَىَّ وَلَمْ يُوحَ إِلَيْهِ شَىْءٌ وَمَن قَالَ سَأُنزِلُ مِثْلَ مَآ أَنزَلَ ٱللَّهُ وَلَوْ تَرَىٰٓ إِذِ ٱلظَّٰلِمُونَ فِى غَمَرَٰتِ ٱلْمَوْتِ وَٱلْمَلَٰٓئِكَةُ بَاسِطُوٓاْ أَيْدِيهِمْ أَخْرِجُوٓاْ أَنفُسَكُمُ ٱلْيَوْمَ تُجْزَوْنَ عَذَابَ ٱلْهُونِ بِمَا كُنتُمْ تَقُولُونَ عَلَى ٱللَّهِ غَيْرَ ٱلْحَقِّ وَكُنتُمْ عَنْ ءَايَٰتِهِۦ تَسْتَكْبِرُونَ (٩٣) وَلَقَدْ جِئْتُمُونَا فُرَٰدَىٰ كَمَا خَلَقْنَٰكُمْ أَوَّلَ مَرَّةٍ وَتَرَكْتُم مَّا خَوَّلْنَٰكُمْ وَرَآءَ ظُهُورِكُمْ وَمَا نَرَىٰ مَعَكُمْ شُفَعَآءَكُمُ ٱلَّذِينَ زَعَمْتُمْ أَنَّهُمْ فِيكُمْ شُرَكَٰٓؤُاْ لَقَد تَّقَطَّعَ بَيْنَكُمْ وَضَلَّ عَنكُم مَّا كُنتُمْ تَزْعُمُونَ (٩٤)

And who is more unjust than one who invents a lie about Allah or says, "It has been inspired to me," while nothing has been inspired to him, and one who says, "I will reveal [something] like what Allah revealed." And if you could but see when the wrongdoers are in the overwhelming pangs of death while the angels extend their hands, [saying], "Discharge your souls! Today you will be awarded the punishment of [extreme] humiliation for what you used to say against

Allah other than the truth and [that] you
were, toward His verses, being arrogant."
(93) [It will be said to them], "And you have
certainly come to Us alone as We created
you the first time, and you have left
whatever We bestowed upon you behind
you. And We do not see with you your
'intercessors' which you claimed that they
were among you associates [of Allah]. It has
[all] been severed between you, and lost from
you is what you used to claim." (94)

Quran 6:100-101

وَجَعَلُواْ لِلَّهِ شُرَكَآءَ ٱلْجِنَّ وَخَلَقَهُمْۖ وَخَرَقُواْ لَهُۥ بَنِينَ وَبَنَٰتٍ
بِغَيْرِ عِلْمٍۚ سُبْحَٰنَهُۥ وَتَعَٰلَىٰ عَمَّا يَصِفُونَ (١٠٠) بَدِيعُ
ٱلسَّمَٰوَٰتِ وَٱلْأَرْضِۖ أَنَّىٰ يَكُونُ لَهُۥ وَلَدٌ وَلَمْ تَكُن لَّهُۥ
صَٰحِبَةٌۖ وَخَلَقَ كُلَّ شَىْءٍۖ وَهُوَ بِكُلِّ شَىْءٍ عَلِيمٌ (١٠١)

But they have attributed to Allah partners -
the jinn, while He has created them - and
have fabricated for Him sons and daughters.
Exalted is He and high above what they

describe (100) [He is] Originator of the heavens and the earth. How could He have a son when He does not have a companion and He created all things? And He is, of all things, Knowing. (101)

Quran 6:144

وَمِنَ ٱلْإِبِلِ ٱثْنَيْنِ وَمِنَ ٱلْبَقَرِ ٱثْنَيْنِ ۗ قُلْ ءَآلذَّكَرَيْنِ حَرَّمَ أَمِ ٱلْأُنثَيَيْنِ أَمَّا ٱشْتَمَلَتْ عَلَيْهِ أَرْحَامُ ٱلْأُنثَيَيْنِ ۖ أَمْ كُنتُمْ شُهَدَآءَ إِذْ وَصَّىٰكُمُ ٱللَّهُ بِهَٰذَا ۚ فَمَنْ أَظْلَمُ مِمَّنِ ٱفْتَرَىٰ عَلَى ٱللَّهِ كَذِبًا لِّيُضِلَّ ٱلنَّاسَ بِغَيْرِ عِلْمٍ ۗ إِنَّ ٱللَّهَ لَا يَهْدِى ٱلْقَوْمَ ٱلظَّٰلِمِينَ (١٤٤)

And of the camels, two and of the cattle, two. Say, "Is it the two males He has forbidden or the two females or that which the wombs of the two females contain? Or were you witnesses when Allah charged you with this? Then who is more unjust than one who invents a lie about Allah to mislead the people by [something] other than knowledge? Indeed, Allah does not guide the wrongdoing people." (144)

Quran 6:148-150

سَيَقُولُ ٱلَّذِينَ أَشْرَكُواْ لَوْ شَاءَ ٱللَّهُ مَآ أَشْرَكْنَا وَلَآ ءَابَآؤُنَا وَلَا حَرَّمْنَا مِن شَىْءٍ كَذَٰلِكَ كَذَّبَ ٱلَّذِينَ مِن قَبْلِهِمْ حَتَّىٰ ذَاقُواْ بَأْسَنَا قُلْ هَلْ عِندَكُم مِّنْ عِلْمٍ فَتُخْرِجُوهُ لَنَآ إِن تَتَّبِعُونَ إِلَّا ٱلظَّنَّ وَإِنْ أَنتُمْ إِلَّا تَخْرُصُونَ (١٤٨) قُلْ فَلِلَّهِ ٱلْحُجَّةُ ٱلْبَٰلِغَةُ فَلَوْ شَاءَ لَهَدَىٰكُمْ أَجْمَعِينَ (١٤٩) قُلْ هَلُمَّ شُهَدَآءَكُمُ ٱلَّذِينَ يَشْهَدُونَ أَنَّ ٱللَّهَ حَرَّمَ هَٰذَا فَإِن شَهِدُواْ فَلَا تَشْهَدْ مَعَهُمْ وَلَا تَتَّبِعْ أَهْوَآءَ ٱلَّذِينَ كَذَّبُواْ بِـَٔايَٰتِنَا وَٱلَّذِينَ لَا يُؤْمِنُونَ بِٱلْأَخِرَةِ وَهُم بِرَبِّهِمْ يَعْدِلُونَ (١٥٠)

Those who associated with Allah will say, "If Allah had willed, we would not have associated [anything] and neither would our fathers, nor would we have prohibited anything." Likewise did those before deny until they tasted Our punishment. Say, "Do you have any knowledge that you can produce for us? You follow not except assumption, and you are not but falsifying." (148) Say, "With Allah is the far-reaching argument. If He had willed, He would have guided you all." (149) Say, [O

Muhammad], "Bring forward your witnesses who will testify that Allah has prohibited this." And if they testify, do not testify with them. And do not follow the desires of those who deny Our verses and those who do not believe in the Hereafter, while they equate [others] with their Lord. (150)

Quran 7:20-22

فَوَسْوَسَ لَهُمَا ٱلشَّيْطَـٰنُ لِيُبْدِىَ لَهُمَا مَا وُۥرِىَ عَنْهُمَا مِن سَوْءَٰتِهِمَا وَقَالَ مَا نَهَٰكُمَا رَبُّكُمَا عَنْ هَٰذِهِ ٱلشَّجَرَةِ إِلَّآ أَن تَكُونَا مَلَكَيْنِ أَوْ تَكُونَا مِنَ ٱلْخَـٰلِدِينَ (٢٠) وَقَاسَمَهُمَآ إِنِّى لَكُمَا لَمِنَ ٱلنَّـٰصِحِينَ (٢١) فَدَلَّىٰهُمَا بِغُرُورٍۚ فَلَمَّا ذَاقَا ٱلشَّجَرَةَ بَدَتْ لَهُمَا سَوْءَٰتُهُمَا وَطَفِقَا يَخْصِفَانِ عَلَيْهِمَا مِن وَرَقِ ٱلْجَنَّةِۖ وَنَادَىٰهُمَا رَبُّهُمَآ أَلَمْ أَنْهَكُمَا عَن تِلْكُمَا ٱلشَّجَرَةِ وَأَقُل لَّكُمَآ إِنَّ ٱلشَّيْطَـٰنَ لَكُمَا عَدُوٌّ مُّبِينٌ (٢٢)

But Satan whispered to them to make apparent to them that which was concealed from them of their private parts. He said, "Your Lord did not forbid you this tree except that you become angels or become of the immortal." (20) And he swore [by Allah] to them, "Indeed, I am to you from among the sincere advisors." (21) So he made them fall, through deception. And when they tasted of the tree, their private parts became apparent to them, and they began to fasten together over themselves from the leaves of Paradise. And their Lord called to them, "Did I not forbid you from that tree and tell you that Satan is to you a clear enemy?" (22)

Quran 7:37-38

فَمَنْ أَظْلَمُ مِمَّنِ ٱفْتَرَىٰ عَلَى ٱللَّهِ كَذِبًا أَوْ كَذَّبَ بِـَٔايَٰتِهِۦٓ أُوْلَٰٓئِكَ يَنَالُهُمْ نَصِيبُهُم مِّنَ ٱلْكِتَٰبِ حَتَّىٰٓ إِذَا جَآءَتْهُمْ رُسُلُنَا يَتَوَفَّوْنَهُمْ قَالُوٓاْ أَيْنَ مَا كُنتُمْ تَدْعُونَ مِن دُونِ ٱللَّهِ قَالُواْ ضَلُّواْ عَنَّا وَشَهِدُواْ عَلَىٰٓ أَنفُسِهِمْ أَنَّهُمْ كَانُواْ كَٰفِرِينَ (٣٧) قَالَ ٱدْخُلُواْ فِىٓ أُمَمٍ قَدْ خَلَتْ مِن قَبْلِكُم مِّنَ ٱلْجِنِّ وَٱلْإِنسِ فِى ٱلنَّارِ كُلَّمَا دَخَلَتْ أُمَّةٌ لَّعَنَتْ أُخْتَهَا حَتَّىٰٓ إِذَا ٱدَّارَكُواْ فِيهَا جَمِيعًا قَالَتْ أُخْرَىٰهُمْ لِأُولَىٰهُمْ رَبَّنَا هَٰٓؤُلَآءِ أَضَلُّونَا فَـَٔاتِهِمْ عَذَابًا ضِعْفًا مِّنَ ٱلنَّارِ قَالَ لِكُلٍّ ضِعْفٌ وَلَٰكِن لَّا تَعْلَمُونَ (٣٨)

And who is more unjust than one who invents about Allah a lie or denies His verses? Those will attain their portion of the decree until when Our messengers come to them to take them in death, they will say, "Where are those you used to invoke besides Allah?" They will say, "They have departed from us," and will bear witness against themselves that they were disbelievers. (37) [Allah] will say, "Enter among nations which had passed on before you of jinn and mankind into the Fire." Every time a nation enters, it will curse its sister until, when they have all overtaken one another therein, the last of them will say about the first of them "Our Lord, these had misled us, so give them a double punishment of the Fire. He will say, "For each is double, but you do not know." (38)

Quran 7:162

فَبَدَّلَ ٱلَّذِينَ ظَلَمُوا۟ قَوْلًا غَيْرَ ٱلَّذِى قِيلَ لَهُمْ فَأَرْسَلْنَا عَلَيْهِمْ رِجْزًا مِّنَ ٱلسَّمَآءِ بِمَا كَانُوا۟ يَظْلِمُونَ (١٦٢)

But those who wronged among them changed [the words] to a statement other than that which had been said to them. So We sent upon them a punishment from the sky for the wrong that they were doing. (162)

Quran 9:12-13

وَإِن نَّكَثُوٓا۟ أَيْمَـٰنَهُم مِّنۢ بَعْدِ عَهْدِهِمْ وَطَعَنُوا۟ فِى دِينِكُمْ فَقَـٰتِلُوٓا۟ أَئِمَّةَ ٱلْكُفْرِ إِنَّهُمْ لَآ أَيْمَـٰنَ لَهُمْ لَعَلَّهُمْ يَنتَهُونَ (١٢) أَلَا تُقَـٰتِلُونَ قَوْمًا نَّكَثُوٓا۟ أَيْمَـٰنَهُمْ وَهَمُّوا۟ بِإِخْرَاجِ ٱلرَّسُولِ وَهُم بَدَءُوكُمْ أَوَّلَ مَرَّةٍ أَتَخْشَوْنَهُمْ فَٱللَّهُ أَحَقُّ أَن تَخْشَوْهُ إِن كُنتُم مُّؤْمِنِينَ (١٣)

And if they break their oaths after their treaty and defame your religion, then fight the leaders of disbelief, for indeed, there are no oaths [sacred] to them; [fight them that] they might cease. (12) Would you not fight a people who broke their oaths and determined to expel the Messenger, and they had begun [the attack upon] you the first time? Do you fear them? But Allah has more right that you should fear Him, if you are [truly] believers. (13)

Quran 9:90

وَجَاءَ ٱلْمُعَذِّرُونَ مِنَ ٱلْأَعْرَابِ لِيُؤْذَنَ لَهُمْ وَقَعَدَ ٱلَّذِينَ كَذَبُواْ ٱللَّهَ وَرَسُولَهُۥ ۚ سَيُصِيبُ ٱلَّذِينَ كَفَرُواْ مِنْهُمْ عَذَابٌ أَلِيمٌ (٩٠)

And those with excuses among the bedouins came to be permitted [to remain], and they who had lied to Allah and His Messenger sat [at home]. There will strike those who disbelieved among them a painful punishment. (90)

Quran 9:93-96

۞ إِنَّمَا ٱلسَّبِيلُ عَلَى ٱلَّذِينَ يَسْتَـْٔذِنُونَكَ وَهُمْ أَغْنِيَآءُ ۚ رَضُواْ بِأَن يَكُونُواْ مَعَ ٱلْخَوَالِفِ وَطَبَعَ ٱللَّهُ عَلَىٰ قُلُوبِهِمْ فَهُمْ لَا يَعْلَمُونَ (٩٣) يَعْتَذِرُونَ إِلَيْكُمْ إِذَا رَجَعْتُمْ إِلَيْهِمْ ۚ قُل لَّا تَعْتَذِرُواْ لَن نُّؤْمِنَ لَكُمْ قَدْ نَبَّأَنَا ٱللَّهُ مِنْ أَخْبَارِكُمْ ۚ وَسَيَرَى

ٱللَّهُ عَمَلَكُمْ وَرَسُولُهُ ۚ ثُمَّ تُرَدُّونَ إِلَىٰ عَـٰلِمِ ٱلْغَيْبِ وَٱلشَّهَـٰدَةِ فَيُنَبِّئُكُم بِمَا كُنتُمْ تَعْمَلُونَ (٩٤) سَيَحْلِفُونَ بِٱللَّهِ لَكُمْ إِذَا ٱنقَلَبْتُمْ إِلَيْهِمْ لِتُعْرِضُوا۟ عَنْهُمْ ۖ فَأَعْرِضُوا۟ عَنْهُمْ ۖ إِنَّهُمْ رِجْسٌ ۖ وَمَأْوَىٰهُمْ جَهَنَّمُ جَزَآءً بِمَا كَانُوا۟ يَكْسِبُونَ (٩٥) يَحْلِفُونَ لَكُمْ لِتَرْضَوْا۟ عَنْهُمْ ۖ فَإِن تَرْضَوْا۟ عَنْهُمْ فَإِنَّ ٱللَّهَ لَا يَرْضَىٰ عَنِ ٱلْقَوْمِ ٱلْفَـٰسِقِينَ (٩٦)

The cause [for blame] is only upon those who ask permission of you while they are rich. They are satisfied to be with those who stay behind, and Allah has sealed over their hearts, so they do not know. (93) They will make excuses to you when you have returned to them. Say, "Make no excuse - never will we believe you. Allah has already informed us of your news. And Allah will observe your deeds, and [so will] His Messenger; then you will be taken back to the Knower of the unseen and the witnessed, and He will inform you of what you used to do." (94) They will swear by Allah to you when you return to them that you would

*leave them alone. So leave them alone;
indeed they are evil; and their refuge is Hell
as recompense for what they had been
earning. (95) They swear to you so that you
might be satisfied with them. But if you
should be satisfied with them - indeed, Allah
is not satisfied with a defiantly disobedient
people. (96)*

Quran 9:107-110

وَٱلَّذِينَ ٱتَّخَذُوا۟ مَسْجِدًا ضِرَارًا وَكُفْرًا وَتَفْرِيقًۢا بَيْنَ
ٱلْمُؤْمِنِينَ وَإِرْصَادًا لِّمَنْ حَارَبَ ٱللَّهَ وَرَسُولَهُۥ مِن قَبْلُ
وَلَيَحْلِفُنَّ إِنْ أَرَدْنَآ إِلَّا ٱلْحُسْنَىٰ وَٱللَّهُ يَشْهَدُ إِنَّهُمْ لَكَٰذِبُونَ
(١٠٧) لَا تَقُمْ فِيهِ أَبَدًا لَّمَسْجِدٌ أُسِّسَ عَلَى ٱلتَّقْوَىٰ مِنْ أَوَّلِ
يَوْمٍ أَحَقُّ أَن تَقُومَ فِيهِ فِيهِ رِجَالٌ يُحِبُّونَ أَن يَتَطَهَّرُوا۟ وَٱللَّهُ
يُحِبُّ ٱلْمُطَّهِّرِينَ (١٠٨) أَفَمَنْ أَسَّسَ بُنْيَٰنَهُۥ عَلَىٰ تَقْوَىٰ مِنَ
ٱللَّهِ وَرِضْوَٰنٍ خَيْرٌ أَم مَّنْ أَسَّسَ بُنْيَٰنَهُۥ عَلَىٰ شَفَا جُرُفٍ
هَارٍ فَٱنْهَارَ بِهِۦ فِى نَارِ جَهَنَّمَ وَٱللَّهُ لَا يَهْدِى ٱلْقَوْمَ ٱلظَّٰلِمِينَ
(١٠٩) لَا يَزَالُ بُنْيَٰنُهُمُ ٱلَّذِى بَنَوْا۟ رِيبَةً فِى قُلُوبِهِمْ إِلَّآ أَن
تَقَطَّعَ قُلُوبُهُمْ وَٱللَّهُ عَلِيمٌ حَكِيمٌ (١١٠)

*And [there are] those [hypocrites] who took
for themselves a mosque for causing harm*

164

and disbelief and division among the believers and as a station for whoever had warred against Allah and His Messenger before. And they will surely swear, "We intended only the best." And Allah testifies that indeed they are liars. (107) Do not stand [for prayer] within it - ever. A mosque founded on righteousness from the first day is more worthy for you to stand in. Within it are men who love to purify themselves; and Allah loves those who purify themselves. (108) Then is one who laid the foundation of his building on righteousness [with fear] from Allah and [seeking] His approval better or one who laid the foundation of his building on the edge of a bank about to collapse, so it collapsed with him into the fire of Hell? And Allah does not guide the wrongdoing people. (109) Their building which they built will not cease to be a [cause of] skepticism in their hearts until their

*hearts are stopped. And Allah is Knowing
and Wise. (110)*

Quran 9:119

يَـٰٓأَيُّهَا ٱلَّذِينَ ءَامَنُوا۟ ٱتَّقُوا۟ ٱللَّهَ وَكُونُوا۟ مَعَ ٱلصَّـٰدِقِينَ (١١٩)

*O you who have believed, fear Allah and be
with those who are true. (119)*

Quran 10:27-30

وَٱلَّذِينَ كَسَبُوا۟ ٱلسَّيِّـَٔاتِ جَزَآءُ سَيِّئَةٍۭ بِمِثْلِهَا وَتَرْهَقُهُمْ ذِلَّةٌ مَّا
لَهُم مِّنَ ٱللَّهِ مِنْ عَاصِمٍ كَأَنَّمَآ أُغْشِيَتْ وُجُوهُهُمْ قِطَعًا مِّنَ
ٱلَّيْلِ مُظْلِمًا أُو۟لَـٰٓئِكَ أَصْحَـٰبُ ٱلنَّارِ هُمْ فِيهَا خَـٰلِدُونَ
(٢٧) وَيَوْمَ نَحْشُرُهُمْ جَمِيعًا ثُمَّ نَقُولُ لِلَّذِينَ أَشْرَكُوا۟ مَكَانَكُمْ
أَنتُمْ وَشُرَكَآؤُكُمْ فَزَيَّلْنَا بَيْنَهُمْ وَقَالَ شُرَكَآؤُهُم مَّا كُنتُمْ إِيَّانَا
تَعْبُدُونَ (٢٨) فَكَفَىٰ بِٱللَّهِ شَهِيدًۢا بَيْنَنَا وَبَيْنَكُمْ إِن كُنَّا عَنْ
عِبَادَتِكُمْ لَغَـٰفِلِينَ (٢٩) هُنَالِكَ تَبْلُوا۟ كُلُّ نَفْسٍ مَّآ أَسْلَفَتْ
وَرُدُّوٓا۟ إِلَى ٱللَّهِ مَوْلَـٰهُمُ ٱلْحَقِّ وَضَلَّ عَنْهُم مَّا كَانُوا۟ يَفْتَرُونَ
(٣٠)

*But they who have earned [blame for] evil
doings - the recompense of an evil deed is its
equivalent, and humiliation will cover them.*

They will have from Allah no protector. It will be as if their faces are covered with pieces of the night - so dark [are they]. Those are the companions of the Fire; they will abide therein eternally. (27) And [mention, O Muhammad], the Day We will gather them all together - then We will say to those who associated others with Allah, "[Remain in] your place, you and your 'partners.' " Then We will separate them, and their "partners" will say, "You did not used to worship us, (28) And sufficient is Allah as a witness between us and you that we were of your worship unaware." (29) There, [on that Day], every soul will be put to trial for what it did previously, and they will be returned to Allah, their master, the Truth, and lost from them is whatever they used to invent. (30)

Quran 10:68-69

قَالُوا۟ ٱتَّخَذَ ٱللَّهُ وَلَدًا ۗ سُبْحَـٰنَهُۥ ۖ هُوَ ٱلْغَنِىُّ ۖ لَهُۥ مَا فِى ٱلسَّمَـٰوَٰتِ وَمَا فِى ٱلْأَرْضِ ۚ إِنْ عِندَكُم مِّن سُلْطَـٰنٍۭ بِهَـٰذَآ ۚ أَتَقُولُونَ عَلَى ٱللَّهِ مَا لَا تَعْلَمُونَ (٦٨) قُلْ إِنَّ ٱلَّذِينَ يَفْتَرُونَ عَلَى ٱللَّهِ ٱلْكَذِبَ لَا يُفْلِحُونَ (٦٩)

They have said, "Allah has taken a son."
Exalted is He; He is the [one] Free of need.
To Him belongs whatever is in the heavens
and whatever is in the earth. You have no
authority for this [claim]. Do you say about
Allah that which you do not know?
(68) Say, "Indeed, those who invent
falsehood about Allah will not succeed." (69)

Quran 10:81-82

فَلَمَّآ أَلْقَوْا۟ قَالَ مُوسَىٰ مَا جِئْتُم بِهِ ٱلسِّحْرُ ۖ إِنَّ ٱللَّهَ سَيُبْطِلُهُۥٓ ۖ إِنَّ ٱللَّهَ لَا يُصْلِحُ عَمَلَ ٱلْمُفْسِدِينَ (٨١) وَيُحِقُّ ٱللَّهُ ٱلْحَقَّ بِكَلِمَـٰتِهِۦ ۖ وَلَوْ كَرِهَ ٱلْمُجْرِمُونَ (٨٢)

And when they had thrown, Moses said,
"What you have brought is [only] magic.
Indeed, Allah will expose its worthlessness.
Indeed, Allah does not amend the work of

corrupters. (81) And Allah will establish the truth by His words, even if the criminals dislike it." (82)

Quran 11:17-22

أَفَمَن كَانَ عَلَىٰ بَيِّنَةٍ مِّن رَّبِّهِۦ وَيَتْلُوهُ شَاهِدٌ مِّنْهُ وَمِن قَبْلِهِۦ كِتَـٰبُ مُوسَىٰٓ إِمَامًا وَرَحْمَةً أُو۟لَـٰٓئِكَ يُؤْمِنُونَ بِهِۦ وَمَن يَكْفُرْ بِهِۦ مِنَ ٱلْأَحْزَابِ فَٱلنَّارُ مَوْعِدُهُۥ فَلَا تَكُ فِى مِرْيَةٍ مِّنْهُ إِنَّهُ ٱلْحَقُّ مِن رَّبِّكَ وَلَـٰكِنَّ أَكْثَرَ ٱلنَّاسِ لَا يُؤْمِنُونَ (١٧) وَمَنْ أَظْلَمُ مِمَّنِ ٱفْتَرَىٰ عَلَى ٱللَّهِ كَذِبًا أُو۟لَـٰٓئِكَ يُعْرَضُونَ عَلَىٰ رَبِّهِمْ وَيَقُولُ ٱلْأَشْهَـٰدُ هَـٰٓؤُلَآءِ ٱلَّذِينَ كَذَبُوا۟ عَلَىٰ رَبِّهِمْ أَلَا لَعْنَةُ ٱللَّهِ عَلَى ٱلظَّـٰلِمِينَ (١٨) ٱلَّذِينَ يَصُدُّونَ عَن سَبِيلِ ٱللَّهِ وَيَبْغُونَهَا عِوَجًا وَهُم بِٱلْأَخِرَةِ هُمْ كَـٰفِرُونَ (١٩) أُو۟لَـٰٓئِكَ لَمْ يَكُونُوا۟ مُعْجِزِينَ فِى ٱلْأَرْضِ وَمَا كَانَ لَهُم مِّن دُونِ ٱللَّهِ مِنْ أَوْلِيَآءَ يُضَـٰعَفُ لَهُمُ ٱلْعَذَابُ مَا كَانُوا۟ يَسْتَطِيعُونَ ٱلسَّمْعَ وَمَا كَانُوا۟ يُبْصِرُونَ (٢٠) أُو۟لَـٰٓئِكَ ٱلَّذِينَ خَسِرُوٓا۟ أَنفُسَهُمْ وَضَلَّ عَنْهُم مَّا كَانُوا۟ يَفْتَرُونَ (٢١) لَا جَرَمَ أَنَّهُمْ فِى ٱلْأَخِرَةِ هُمُ ٱلْأَخْسَرُونَ (٢٢)

So is one who [stands] upon a clear evidence from his Lord [like the aforementioned]? And a witness from Him follows it, and before it was the Scripture of Moses to lead and as mercy. Those [believers in the former revelations] believe in the Qur'an. But whoever disbelieves in it from the [various] factions - the Fire is his promised destination. So be not in doubt about it. Indeed, it is the truth from your Lord, but most of the people do not believe. (17) And who is more unjust than he who invents a lie about Allah? Those will be presented before their Lord, and the witnesses will say, "These are the ones who lied against their Lord." Unquestionably, the curse of Allah is upon the wrongdoers. (18) Who averted [people] from the way of Allah and sought to make it [seem] deviant while they, concerning the Hereafter, were disbelievers. (19) Those were not causing failure [to Allah] on earth, nor did they have besides Allah any protectors. For them the punishment will be multiplied. They were not able to hear, nor did they see. (20) Those are the ones who will have lost themselves, and lost from them is what they used to invent. (21) Assuredly, it is they in the Hereafter who will be the greatest losers. (22)

Quran 12:25-27

وَٱسْتَبَقَا ٱلْبَابَ وَقَدَّتْ قَمِيصَهُ ۥ مِن دُبُرٍ وَأَلْفَيَا سَيِّدَهَا لَدَا ٱلْبَابِ ۚ قَالَتْ مَا جَزَآءُ مَنْ أَرَادَ بِأَهْلِكَ سُوٓءًا إِلَّآ أَن يُسْجَنَ أَوْ عَذَابٌ أَلِيمٌ (٢٥) قَالَ هِىَ رَٰوَدَتْنِى عَن نَّفْسِى ۚ وَشَهِدَ شَاهِدٌ مِّنْ أَهْلِهَآ إِن كَانَ قَمِيصُهُ ۥ قُدَّ مِن قُبُلٍ فَصَدَقَتْ وَهُوَ مِنَ ٱلْكَٰذِبِينَ (٢٦) وَإِن كَانَ قَمِيصُهُ ۥ قُدَّ مِن دُبُرٍ فَكَذَبَتْ وَهُوَ مِنَ ٱلصَّٰدِقِينَ (٢٧)

And they both raced to the door, and she tore his shirt from the back, and they found her husband at the door. She said, "What is the recompense of one who intended evil for your wife but that he be imprisoned or a painful punishment?" (25) [Joseph] said, "It was she who sought to seduce me." And a witness from her family testified. "If his shirt is torn from the front, then she has told the truth, and he is of the liars. (26) But if *his shirt is torn from the back, then she has lied, and he is of the truthful." (27)*

Quran 16:86-88

وَإِذَا رَءَا ٱلَّذِينَ أَشْرَكُواْ شُرَكَآءَهُمْ قَالُواْ رَبَّنَا هَٰٓؤُلَآءِ شُرَكَآؤُنَا ٱلَّذِينَ كُنَّا نَدْعُواْ مِن دُونِكَۖ فَأَلْقَوْاْ إِلَيْهِمُ ٱلْقَوْلَ إِنَّكُمْ لَكَٰذِبُونَ (٨٦) وَأَلْقَوْاْ إِلَى ٱللَّهِ يَوْمَئِذٍ ٱلسَّلَمَۖ وَضَلَّ عَنْهُم مَّا كَانُواْ يَفْتَرُونَ (٨٧) ٱلَّذِينَ كَفَرُواْ وَصَدُّواْ عَن سَبِيلِ ٱللَّهِ زِدْنَٰهُمْ عَذَابًا فَوْقَ ٱلْعَذَابِ بِمَا كَانُواْ يُفْسِدُونَ (٨٨)

And when those who associated others with Allah see their "partners," they will say," Our Lord, these are our partners [to You] whom we used to invoke besides You." But they will throw at them the statement, "Indeed, you are liars." (86) And they will impart to Allah that Day [their] submission, and lost from them is what they used to invent. (87) Those who disbelieved and averted [others] from the way of Allah - We will increase them in punishment over [their] punishment for what corruption they were causing. (88)

Quran 16:104-105

إِنَّ ٱلَّذِينَ لَا يُؤْمِنُونَ بِـَٔايَٰتِ ٱللَّهِ لَا يَهْدِيهِمُ ٱللَّهُ وَلَهُمْ عَذَابٌ أَلِيمٌ (١٠٤) إِنَّمَا يَفْتَرِى ٱلْكَذِبَ ٱلَّذِينَ لَا يُؤْمِنُونَ بِـَٔايَٰتِ ٱللَّهِ ۖ وَأُوْلَـٰٓئِكَ هُمُ ٱلْكَـٰذِبُونَ (١٠٥)

Indeed, those who do not believe in the verses of Allah - Allah will not guide them, and for them is a painful punishment. (104) They only invent falsehood who do not believe in the verses of Allah, and it is those who are the liars. (105)

Quran 16:116

وَلَا تَقُولُواْ لِمَا تَصِفُ أَلْسِنَتُكُمُ ٱلْكَذِبَ هَٰذَا حَلَٰلٌ وَهَٰذَا حَرَامٌ لِّتَفْتَرُواْ عَلَى ٱللَّهِ ٱلْكَذِبَ ۚ إِنَّ ٱلَّذِينَ يَفْتَرُونَ عَلَى ٱللَّهِ ٱلْكَذِبَ لَا يُفْلِحُونَ (١١٦)

And do not say about what your tongues assert of untruth, "This is lawful and this is unlawful," to invent falsehood about Allah.

Indeed, those who invent falsehood about Allah will not succeed. (116)

Quran 17:81

وَقُلْ جَآءَ ٱلْحَقُّ وَزَهَقَ ٱلْبَٰطِلُ إِنَّ ٱلْبَٰطِلَ كَانَ زَهُوقًا (٨١)

And say, "Truth has come, and falsehood has departed. Indeed is falsehood, [by nature], ever bound to depart." (81)

Quran 18:4-5

وَيُنذِرَ ٱلَّذِينَ قَالُوا۟ ٱتَّخَذَ ٱللَّهُ وَلَدًا (٤) مَّا لَهُم بِهِۦ مِنْ عِلْمٍ وَلَا لِأَبَآئِهِمْ كَبُرَتْ كَلِمَةً تَخْرُجُ مِنْ أَفْوَاهِهِمْ إِن يَقُولُونَ إِلَّا كَذِبًا (٥)

And to warn those who say, "Allah has taken a son." (4) They have no knowledge of it, nor had their fathers. Grave is the word that comes out of their mouths; they speak not except a lie. (5)

Quran 18:14-15

وَرَبَطْنَا عَلَىٰ قُلُوبِهِمْ إِذْ قَامُوا۟ فَقَالُوا۟ رَبُّنَا رَبُّ ٱلسَّمَٰوَٰتِ وَٱلْأَرْضِ لَن نَّدْعُوَا۟ مِن دُونِهِۦٓ إِلَٰهًۭا لَّقَدْ قُلْنَآ إِذًۭا شَطَطًا ﴿١٤﴾ هَٰٓؤُلَآءِ قَوْمُنَا ٱتَّخَذُوا۟ مِن دُونِهِۦٓ ءَالِهَةًۭ لَّوْلَا يَأْتُونَ عَلَيْهِم بِسُلْطَٰنٍۭ بَيِّنٍۢ فَمَنْ أَظْلَمُ مِمَّنِ ٱفْتَرَىٰ عَلَى ٱللَّهِ كَذِبًۭا ﴿١٥﴾

And We made firm their hearts when they stood up and said, "Our Lord is the Lord of the heavens and the earth. Never will we invoke besides Him any deity. We would have certainly spoken, then, an excessive transgression. (14) These, our people, have taken besides Him deities. Why do they not bring for [worship of] them a clear authority? And who is more unjust than one who invents about Allah a lie?" (15)

Quran 21:18

بَلْ نَقْذِفُ بِٱلْحَقِّ عَلَى ٱلْبَٰطِلِ فَيَدْمَغُهُۥ فَإِذَا هُوَ زَاهِقٌۭ وَلَكُمُ ٱلْوَيْلُ مِمَّا تَصِفُونَ ﴿١٨﴾

Rather, We dash the truth upon falsehood, and it destroys it, and thereupon it departs.

And for you is destruction from that which you describe. (18)

Quran 22:52-53

وَمَآ أَرْسَلْنَا مِن قَبْلِكَ مِن رَّسُولٍ وَلَا نَبِيٍّ إِلَّآ إِذَا تَمَنَّىٰٓ أَلْقَى
ٱلشَّيْطَـٰنُ فِىٓ أُمْنِيَّتِهِۦ فَيَنسَخُ ٱللَّهُ مَا يُلْقِى ٱلشَّيْطَـٰنُ ثُمَّ يُحْكِمُ
ٱللَّهُ ءَايَـٰتِهِۦ وَٱللَّهُ عَلِيمٌ حَكِيمٌ (٥٢) لِّيَجْعَلَ مَا يُلْقِى ٱلشَّيْطَـٰنُ
فِتْنَةً لِّلَّذِينَ فِى قُلُوبِهِم مَّرَضٌ وَٱلْقَاسِيَةِ قُلُوبُهُمْ وَإِنَّ ٱلظَّـٰلِمِينَ
لَفِى شِقَاقٍ بَعِيدٍ (٥٣)

And We did not send before you any messenger or prophet except that when he spoke [or recited], Satan threw into it [some misunderstanding]. But Allah abolishes that which Satan throws in; then Allah makes precise His verses. And Allah is Knowing and Wise. (52) [That is] so He may make what Satan throws in a trial for those within whose hearts is disease and those hard of heart. And indeed, the wrongdoers are in extreme dissension. (53)

Quran 24:4-21

وَٱلَّذِينَ يَرْمُونَ ٱلْمُحْصَنَـٰتِ ثُمَّ لَمْ يَأْتُوا۟ بِأَرْبَعَةِ شُهَدَآءَ فَٱجْلِدُوهُمْ ثَمَـٰنِينَ جَلْدَةً وَلَا تَقْبَلُوا۟ لَهُمْ شَهَـٰدَةً أَبَدًا وَأُو۟لَـٰٓئِكَ هُمُ ٱلْفَـٰسِقُونَ (٤) إِلَّا ٱلَّذِينَ تَابُوا۟ مِنۢ بَعْدِ ذَٰلِكَ وَأَصْلَحُوا۟ فَإِنَّ ٱللَّهَ غَفُورٌ رَّحِيمٌ (٥) وَٱلَّذِينَ يَرْمُونَ أَزْوَٰجَهُمْ وَلَمْ يَكُن لَّهُمْ شُهَدَآءُ إِلَّآ أَنفُسُهُمْ فَشَهَـٰدَةُ أَحَدِهِمْ أَرْبَعُ شَهَـٰدَٰتٍۭ بِٱللَّهِ إِنَّهُۥ لَمِنَ ٱلصَّـٰدِقِينَ (٦) وَٱلْخَـٰمِسَةُ أَنَّ لَعْنَتَ ٱللَّهِ عَلَيْهِ إِن كَانَ مِنَ ٱلْكَـٰذِبِينَ (٧) وَيَدْرَؤُا۟ عَنْهَا ٱلْعَذَابَ أَن تَشْهَدَ أَرْبَعَ شَهَـٰدَٰتٍۭ بِٱللَّهِ إِنَّهُۥ لَمِنَ ٱلْكَـٰذِبِينَ (٨) وَٱلْخَـٰمِسَةَ أَنَّ غَضَبَ ٱللَّهِ عَلَيْهَآ إِن كَانَ مِنَ ٱلصَّـٰدِقِينَ (٩) وَلَوْلَا فَضْلُ ٱللَّهِ عَلَيْكُمْ وَرَحْمَتُهُۥ وَأَنَّ ٱللَّهَ تَوَّابٌ حَكِيمٌ (١٠) إِنَّ ٱلَّذِينَ جَآءُو بِٱلْإِفْكِ عُصْبَةٌ مِّنكُمْ لَا تَحْسَبُوهُ شَرًّا لَّكُم بَلْ هُوَ خَيْرٌ لَّكُمْ لِكُلِّ ٱمْرِئٍ مِّنْهُم مَّا ٱكْتَسَبَ مِنَ ٱلْإِثْمِ وَٱلَّذِى تَوَلَّىٰ كِبْرَهُۥ مِنْهُمْ لَهُۥ عَذَابٌ عَظِيمٌ (١١) لَّوْلَآ إِذْ سَمِعْتُمُوهُ ظَنَّ ٱلْمُؤْمِنُونَ وَٱلْمُؤْمِنَـٰتُ بِأَنفُسِهِمْ خَيْرًا وَقَالُوا۟ هَـٰذَآ إِفْكٌ مُّبِينٌ (١٢) لَّوْلَا جَآءُو عَلَيْهِ بِأَرْبَعَةِ شُهَدَآءَ فَإِذْ لَمْ يَأْتُوا۟ بِٱلشُّهَدَآءِ فَأُو۟لَـٰٓئِكَ عِندَ ٱللَّهِ هُمُ ٱلْكَـٰذِبُونَ (١٣) وَلَوْلَا فَضْلُ ٱللَّهِ عَلَيْكُمْ وَرَحْمَتُهُۥ فِى ٱلدُّنْيَا وَٱلْآخِرَةِ لَمَسَّكُمْ فِى مَآ أَفَضْتُمْ فِيهِ عَذَابٌ عَظِيمٌ (١٤) إِذْ تَلَقَّوْنَهُۥ بِأَلْسِنَتِكُمْ وَتَقُولُونَ بِأَفْوَاهِكُم مَّا لَيْسَ لَكُم بِهِۦ عِلْمٌ وَتَحْسَبُونَهُۥ هَيِّنًا وَهُوَ عِندَ ٱللَّهِ عَظِيمٌ (١٥) وَلَوْلَآ إِذْ سَمِعْتُمُوهُ قُلْتُم مَّا يَكُونُ لَنَآ أَن نَّتَكَلَّمَ بِهَـٰذَا سُبْحَـٰنَكَ هَـٰذَا بُهْتَـٰنٌ عَظِيمٌ (١٦) يَعِظُكُمُ ٱللَّهُ أَن تَعُودُوا۟ لِمِثْلِهِۦٓ أَبَدًا إِن كُنتُم مُّؤْمِنِينَ (١٧) وَيُبَيِّنُ ٱللَّهُ لَكُمُ ٱلْآيَـٰتِ وَٱللَّهُ عَلِيمٌ حَكِيمٌ (١٨) إِنَّ ٱلَّذِينَ يُحِبُّونَ أَن تَشِيعَ ٱلْفَـٰحِشَةُ

فِى ٱلَّذِينَ ءَامَنُواْ لَهُمْ عَذَابٌ أَلِيمٌ فِى ٱلدُّنْيَا وَٱلْأَخِرَةِ وَٱللَّهُ يَعْلَمُ وَأَنتُمْ لَا تَعْلَمُونَ ﴿١٩﴾ وَلَوْلَا فَضْلُ ٱللَّهِ عَلَيْكُمْ وَرَحْمَتُهُ وَأَنَّ ٱللَّهَ رَءُوفٌ رَّحِيمٌ ﴿٢٠﴾ ۞ يَـٰٓأَيُّهَا ٱلَّذِينَ ءَامَنُواْ لَا تَتَّبِعُواْ خُطُوَٰتِ ٱلشَّيْطَـٰنِ وَمَن يَتَّبِعْ خُطُوَٰتِ ٱلشَّيْطَـٰنِ فَإِنَّهُۥ يَأْمُرُ بِٱلْفَحْشَآءِ وَٱلْمُنكَرِ وَلَوْلَا فَضْلُ ٱللَّهِ عَلَيْكُمْ وَرَحْمَتُهُۥ مَا زَكَىٰ مِنكُم مِّنْ أَحَدٍ أَبَدًا وَلَـٰكِنَّ ٱللَّهَ يُزَكِّى مَن يَشَآءُ وَٱللَّهُ سَمِيعٌ عَلِيمٌ ﴿٢١﴾

And those who accuse chaste women and then do not produce four witnesses - lash them with eighty lashes and do not accept from them testimony ever after. And those are the defiantly disobedient, (4) Except for those who repent thereafter and reform, for indeed, Allah is Forgiving and Merciful. (5) And those who accuse their wives [of adultery] and have no witnesses except themselves - then the witness of one of them [shall be] four testimonies [swearing] by Allah that indeed, he is of the truthful. (6) And the fifth [oath will be] that the curse of Allah be upon him if he should be among *the liars. (7) But it will prevent punishment from her if she gives four testimonies [swearing] by Allah that indeed, he is of the liars. (8) And the fifth [oath will be] that the wrath of Allah be upon her if he was of the truthful. (9) And if not for the favor of Allah upon you and His mercy... and because Allah is Accepting of repentance and Wise. (10) Indeed, those who came with falsehood are a group among you. Do not think it bad for you; rather it is good for you. For every person among them is what [punishment] he has earned from the sin, and he who took upon himself the greater portion thereof - for him is a great punishment. (11) Why, when you heard it, did not the believing men and believing women think good of one another and say, "This is an obvious falsehood"? (12) Why did they [who slandered] not produce for it four witnesses? And when they do not produce the witnesses, then it is they, in the sight of Allah, who are the liars.*

(13) And if it had not been for the favor of Allah upon you and His mercy in this world and the Hereafter, you would have been touched for that [lie] in which you were involved by a great punishment (14) When you received it with your tongues and said with your mouths that of which you had no knowledge and thought it was insignificant while it was, in the sight of Allah, tremendous. (15) And why, when you heard it, did you not say, "It is not for us to speak of this. Exalted are You, [O Allah]; this is a great slander"? (16) Allah warns you against returning to the likes of this [conduct], ever, if you should be believers. (17) And Allah makes clear to you the verses, and Allah is Knowing and Wise. (18) Indeed, those who like that immorality should be spread [or publicized] among those who have believed will have a painful punishment in this world and the Hereafter. And Allah knows and you do not know.

(19) And if it had not been for the favor of Allah upon you and His mercy... and because Allah is Kind and Merciful. (20) O you who have believed, do not follow the footsteps of Satan. And whoever follows the footsteps of Satan - indeed, he enjoins immorality and wrongdoing. And if not for the favor of Allah upon you and His mercy, not one of you would have been pure, ever, but Allah purifies whom He wills, and Allah is Hearing and Knowing. (21)

Quran 24:23-26

إِنَّ ٱلَّذِينَ يَرْمُونَ ٱلْمُحْصَنَـٰتِ ٱلْغَـٰفِلَـٰتِ ٱلْمُؤْمِنَـٰتِ لُعِنُوا۟ فِى ٱلدُّنْيَا وَٱلْءَاخِرَةِ وَلَهُمْ عَذَابٌ عَظِيمٌ (٢٣) يَوْمَ تَشْهَدُ عَلَيْهِمْ أَلْسِنَتُهُمْ وَأَيْدِيهِمْ وَأَرْجُلُهُم بِمَا كَانُوا۟ يَعْمَلُونَ (٢٤) يَوْمَئِذٍ يُوَفِّيهِمُ ٱللَّهُ دِينَهُمُ ٱلْحَقَّ وَيَعْلَمُونَ أَنَّ ٱللَّهَ هُوَ ٱلْحَقُّ ٱلْمُبِينُ (٢٥) ٱلْخَبِيثَـٰتُ لِلْخَبِيثِينَ وَٱلْخَبِيثُونَ لِلْخَبِيثَـٰتِ وَٱلطَّيِّبَـٰتُ لِلطَّيِّبِينَ وَٱلطَّيِّبُونَ لِلطَّيِّبَـٰتِ أُو۟لَـٰٓئِكَ مُبَرَّءُونَ مِمَّا يَقُولُونَ لَهُم مَّغْفِرَةٌ وَرِزْقٌ كَرِيمٌ (٢٦)

Indeed, those who [falsely] accuse chaste, unaware and believing women are cursed in this world and the Hereafter; and they will have a great punishment (23) On a Day when their tongues, their hands and their feet will bear witness against them as to what they used to do. (24) That Day, Allah will pay them in full their deserved recompense, and they will know that it is Allah who is the perfect in justice. (25) Evil words are for evil men, and evil men are [subjected] to evil words. And good words are for good men, and good men are [an object] of good words. Those [good people] are declared innocent of what the slanderers say. For them is forgiveness and noble provision. (26)

Quran 25:4-6

وَقَالَ ٱلَّذِينَ كَفَرُوٓاْ إِنْ هَٰذَآ إِلَّآ إِفْكٌ ٱفْتَرَىٰهُ وَأَعَانَهُۥ عَلَيْهِ قَوْمٌ ءَاخَرُونَۖ فَقَدْ جَآءُو ظُلْمًا وَزُورًا (٤) وَقَالُوٓاْ أَسَٰطِيرُ ٱلْأَوَّلِينَ ٱكْتَتَبَهَا فَهِىَ تُمْلَىٰ عَلَيْهِ بُكْرَةً وَأَصِيلًا (٥) قُلْ أَنزَلَهُ ٱلَّذِى يَعْلَمُ ٱلسِّرَّ فِى ٱلسَّمَٰوَٰتِ وَٱلْأَرْضِۚ إِنَّهُۥ كَانَ غَفُورًا رَّحِيمًا (٦)

And those who disbelieve say, "This [Qur'an] is not except a falsehood he invented, and another people assisted him in it." But they have committed an injustice and a lie. (4) And they say, "Legends of the former peoples which he has written down, and they are dictated to him morning and afternoon." (5) Say, [O Muhammad], "It has been revealed by He who knows [every] secret within the heavens and the earth. Indeed, He is ever Forgiving and Merciful." (6)

Quran 25:71-72

وَمَن تَابَ وَعَمِلَ صَـٰلِحًا فَإِنَّهُۥ يَتُوبُ إِلَى ٱللَّهِ مَتَابًا (٧١) وَٱلَّذِينَ لَا يَشْهَدُونَ ٱلزُّورَ وَإِذَا مَرُّوا۟ بِٱللَّغْوِ مَرُّوا۟ كِرَامًا (٧٢)

And he who repents and does righteousness does indeed turn to Allah with [accepted] repentance. (71) And [they are] those who do not testify to falsehood, and when they

*pass near ill speech, they pass by with
dignity. (72)*

Quran 26:221-227

هَلْ أُنَبِّئُكُمْ عَلَىٰ مَن تَنَزَّلُ ٱلشَّيَٰطِينُ (٢٢١) تَنَزَّلُ عَلَىٰ كُلِّ
أَفَّاكٍ أَثِيمٍ (٢٢٢) يُلْقُونَ ٱلسَّمْعَ وَأَكْثَرُهُمْ كَٰذِبُونَ
(٢٢٣) وَٱلشُّعَرَآءُ يَتَّبِعُهُمُ ٱلْغَاوُۥنَ (٢٢٤) أَلَمْ تَرَ أَنَّهُمْ فِى
كُلِّ وَادٍ يَهِيمُونَ (٢٢٥) وَأَنَّهُمْ يَقُولُونَ مَا لَا يَفْعَلُونَ
(٢٢٦) إِلَّا ٱلَّذِينَ ءَامَنُواْ وَعَمِلُواْ ٱلصَّٰلِحَٰتِ وَذَكَرُواْ ٱللَّهَ
كَثِيرًا وَٱنتَصَرُواْ مِنۢ بَعْدِ مَا ظُلِمُواۗ وَسَيَعْلَمُ ٱلَّذِينَ ظَلَمُوٓاْ أَىَّ
مُنقَلَبٍ يَنقَلِبُونَ (٢٢٧)

*Shall I inform you upon whom the devils
descend? (221) They descend upon every
sinful liar. (222) They pass on what is heard,
and most of them are liars. (223) And the
poets - [only] the deviators follow them;
(224) See you not that they speak about
every subject (praising people - right or
wrong) in their poetry? (225) And that they
say what they do not do? - (226) Except
those [poets] who believe and do righteous
deeds and remember Allah often and defend*

[the Muslims] after they were wronged. And those who have wronged are going to know to what [kind of] return they will be returned. (227)

Quran 27:27

﴿ قَالَ سَنَنظُرُ أَصَدَقْتَ أَمْ كُنتَ مِنَ ٱلْكَٰذِبِينَ (٢٧)

[Solomon] said, "We will see whether you were truthful or were of the liars. (27)

Quran 27:64-65

أَمَّن يَبْدَؤُاْ ٱلْخَلْقَ ثُمَّ يُعِيدُهُ وَمَن يَرْزُقُكُم مِّنَ ٱلسَّمَآءِ وَٱلْأَرْضِ أَءِلَٰهٌ مَّعَ ٱللَّهِ قُلْ هَاتُواْ بُرْهَٰنَكُمْ إِن كُنتُمْ صَٰدِقِينَ (٦٤) قُل لَّا يَعْلَمُ مَن فِى ٱلسَّمَٰوَٰتِ وَٱلْأَرْضِ ٱلْغَيْبَ إِلَّا ٱللَّهُ وَمَا يَشْعُرُونَ أَيَّانَ يُبْعَثُونَ (٦٥)

Is He [not best] who begins creation and then repeats it and who provides for you from the heaven and earth? Is there a deity with Allah? Say, "Produce your proof, if you should be truthful." (64) Say, "None in the heavens and earth knows the unseen except Allah, and they do not perceive when they will be resurrected." (65)

Quran 29:2-4

أَحَسِبَ ٱلنَّاسُ أَن يُتْرَكُوٓا۟ أَن يَقُولُوٓا۟ ءَامَنَّا وَهُمْ لَا يُفْتَنُونَ
(٢) وَلَقَدْ فَتَنَّا ٱلَّذِينَ مِن قَبْلِهِمْ ۖ فَلَيَعْلَمَنَّ ٱللَّهُ ٱلَّذِينَ صَدَقُوا۟
وَلَيَعْلَمَنَّ ٱلْكَٰذِبِينَ (٣) أَمْ حَسِبَ ٱلَّذِينَ يَعْمَلُونَ ٱلسَّيِّـَٔاتِ أَن
يَسْبِقُونَآ ۚ سَآءَ مَا يَحْكُمُونَ (٤)

Do the people think that they will be left to say, "We believe" and they will not be tried? (2) But We have certainly tried those before them, and Allah will surely make evident those who are truthful, and He will surely make evident the liars. (3) Or do those who do evil deeds think they can outrun Us? Evil is what they judge. (4)

Quran 29:11-13

وَلَيَعْلَمَنَّ ٱللَّهُ ٱلَّذِينَ ءَامَنُوا۟ وَلَيَعْلَمَنَّ ٱلْمُنَٰفِقِينَ (١١) وَقَالَ
ٱلَّذِينَ كَفَرُوا۟ لِلَّذِينَ ءَامَنُوا۟ ٱتَّبِعُوا۟ سَبِيلَنَا وَلْنَحْمِلْ خَطَٰيَٰكُمْ
وَمَا هُم بِحَٰمِلِينَ مِنْ خَطَٰيَٰهُم مِّن شَىْءٍ ۖ إِنَّهُمْ لَكَٰذِبُونَ

(١٢) وَلَيَحْمِلُنَّ أَثْقَالَهُمْ وَأَثْقَالًا مَّعَ أَثْقَالِهِمْ ۖ وَلَيُسْـَٔلُنَّ يَوْمَ
ٱلْقِيَٰمَةِ عَمَّا كَانُوا۟ يَفْتَرُونَ (١٣)

*And Allah will surely make evident those
who believe, and He will surely make
evident the hypocrites. (11) And those who
disbelieve say to those who believe, "Follow
our way, and we will carry your sins." But
they will not carry anything of their sins.
Indeed, they are liars. (12) But they will
surely carry their [own] burdens and [other]
burdens along with their burdens, and they
will surely be questioned on the Day of
Resurrection about what they used to
invent. (13)*

Quran 29:16-17

وَإِبْرَٰهِيمَ إِذْ قَالَ لِقَوْمِهِ ٱعْبُدُوا۟ ٱللَّهَ وَٱتَّقُوهُ ۖ ذَٰلِكُمْ خَيْرٌ لَّكُمْ
إِن كُنتُمْ تَعْلَمُونَ (١٦) إِنَّمَا تَعْبُدُونَ مِن دُونِ ٱللَّهِ أَوْثَٰنًا
وَتَخْلُقُونَ إِفْكًا ۚ إِنَّ ٱلَّذِينَ تَعْبُدُونَ مِن دُونِ ٱللَّهِ لَا يَمْلِكُونَ لَكُمْ
رِزْقًا فَٱبْتَغُوا۟ عِندَ ٱللَّهِ ٱلرِّزْقَ وَٱعْبُدُوهُ وَٱشْكُرُوا۟ لَهُ ۖ إِلَيْهِ
تُرْجَعُونَ (١٧)

And [We sent] Abraham, when he said to his people, "Worship Allah and fear Him. That is best for you, if you should know. (16) You only worship, besides Allah, idols, and you produce a falsehood. Indeed, those you worship besides Allah do not possess for you [the power of] provision. So seek from Allah provision and worship Him and be grateful to Him. To Him you will be returned." (17)

Quran 29:47-52

وَكَذَٰلِكَ أَنزَلْنَآ إِلَيْكَ ٱلْكِتَٰبَ فَٱلَّذِينَ ءَاتَيْنَٰهُمُ ٱلْكِتَٰبَ يُؤْمِنُونَ بِهِۦ ۖ وَمِنْ هَٰٓؤُلَآءِ مَن يُؤْمِنُ بِهِۦ ۚ وَمَا يَجْحَدُ بِـَٔايَٰتِنَآ إِلَّا ٱلْكَٰفِرُونَ (٤٧) وَمَا كُنتَ تَتْلُوا۟ مِن قَبْلِهِۦ مِن كِتَٰبٍ وَلَا تَخُطُّهُۥ بِيَمِينِكَ ۖ إِذًا لَّٱرْتَابَ ٱلْمُبْطِلُونَ (٤٨) بَلْ هُوَ ءَايَٰتٌۢ بَيِّنَٰتٌ فِى صُدُورِ ٱلَّذِينَ أُوتُوا۟ ٱلْعِلْمَ ۚ وَمَا يَجْحَدُ بِـَٔايَٰتِنَآ إِلَّا ٱلظَّٰلِمُونَ (٤٩) وَقَالُوا۟ لَوْلَآ أُنزِلَ عَلَيْهِ ءَايَٰتٌ مِّن رَّبِّهِۦ ۖ قُلْ إِنَّمَا ٱلْـَٔايَٰتُ عِندَ ٱللَّهِ وَإِنَّمَآ أَنَا۠ نَذِيرٌ مُّبِينٌ (٥٠) أَوَلَمْ يَكْفِهِمْ أَنَّآ أَنزَلْنَا عَلَيْكَ ٱلْكِتَٰبَ يُتْلَىٰ عَلَيْهِمْ ۚ إِنَّ فِى ذَٰلِكَ لَرَحْمَةً وَذِكْرَىٰ لِقَوْمٍ يُؤْمِنُونَ (٥١) قُلْ كَفَىٰ بِٱللَّهِ بَيْنِى

وَبَيْنَكُمْ شَهِيدًا ۚ يَعْلَمُ مَا فِى ٱلسَّمَـٰوَٰتِ وَٱلْأَرْضِ ۗ وَٱلَّذِينَ ءَامَنُواْ بِٱلْبَـٰطِلِ وَكَفَرُواْ بِٱللَّهِ أُوْلَـٰئِكَ هُمُ ٱلْخَـٰسِرُونَ (٥٢)

And thus We have sent down to you the Qur'an. And those to whom We [previously] gave the Scripture believe in it. And among these [people of Makkah] are those who believe in it. And none reject Our verses except the disbelievers. (47) And you did not recite before it any scripture, nor did you inscribe one with your right hand. Otherwise the falsifiers would have had [cause for] doubt. (48) Rather, the Qur'an is distinct verses [preserved] within the breasts of those who have been given knowledge. And none reject Our verses except the wrongdoers. (49) But they say, "Why are not signs sent down to him from his Lord?" Say, "The signs are only with Allah, and I am only a clear warner." (50) And is it not sufficient for them that We revealed to you the Book which is recited to them? Indeed in *that is a mercy and reminder for a people who believe. (51) Say, "Sufficient is Allah between me and you as Witness. He knows what is in the heavens and earth. And they who have believed in falsehood and disbelieved in Allah - it is those who are the losers." (52)*

Quran 29:67-68

أَوَلَمْ يَرَوْاْ أَنَّا جَعَلْنَا حَرَمًا ءَامِنًا وَيُتَخَطَّفُ ٱلنَّاسُ مِنْ حَوْلِهِمْ أَفَبِٱلْبَٰطِلِ يُؤْمِنُونَ وَبِنِعْمَةِ ٱللَّهِ يَكْفُرُونَ (٦٧) وَمَنْ أَظْلَمُ مِمَّنِ ٱفْتَرَىٰ عَلَى ٱللَّهِ كَذِبًا أَوْ كَذَّبَ بِٱلْحَقِّ لَمَّا جَآءَهُ ۚ أَلَيْسَ فِى جَهَنَّمَ مَثْوًى لِّلْكَٰفِرِينَ (٦٨)

Have they not seen that We made [Makkah] a safe sanctuary, while people are being taken away all around them? Then in falsehood do they believe, and in the favor of Allah they disbelieve? (67) And who is more unjust than one who invents a lie about Allah or denies the truth when it has come

190

to him? Is there not in Hell a [sufficient]
residence for the disbelievers? (68)

Quran 31:30

ذَٰلِكَ بِأَنَّ ٱللَّهَ هُوَ ٱلْحَقُّ وَأَنَّ مَا يَدْعُونَ مِن دُونِهِ ٱلْبَٰطِلُ وَأَنَّ
ٱللَّهَ هُوَ ٱلْعَلِىُّ ٱلْكَبِيرُ (٣٠)

That is because Allah is the Truth, and that
what they call upon other than Him is
falsehood, and because Allah is the Most
High, the Grand. (30)

Quran 33:4-5

مَّا جَعَلَ ٱللَّهُ لِرَجُلٍ مِّن قَلْبَيْنِ فِى جَوْفِهِ ۚ وَمَا جَعَلَ أَزْوَٰجَكُمُ
ٱلَّـٰٓـِى تُظَٰهِرُونَ مِنْهُنَّ أُمَّهَٰتِكُمْ ۚ وَمَا جَعَلَ أَدْعِيَآءَكُمْ أَبْنَآءَكُمْ ۚ
ذَٰلِكُمْ قَوْلُكُم بِأَفْوَٰهِكُمْ ۖ وَٱللَّهُ يَقُولُ ٱلْحَقَّ وَهُوَ يَهْدِى ٱلسَّبِيلَ
(٤) ٱدْعُوهُمْ لِأَبَآئِهِمْ هُوَ أَقْسَطُ عِندَ ٱللَّهِ ۚ فَإِن لَّمْ تَعْلَمُوٓا۟
ءَابَآءَهُمْ فَإِخْوَٰنُكُمْ فِى ٱلدِّينِ وَمَوَٰلِيكُمْ ۚ وَلَيْسَ عَلَيْكُمْ جُنَاحٌ
فِيمَآ أَخْطَأْتُم بِهِۦ وَلَٰكِن مَّا تَعَمَّدَتْ قُلُوبُكُمْ ۚ وَكَانَ ٱللَّهُ غَفُورًا
رَّحِيمًا (٥)

Allah has not made for a man two hearts in
his interior. And He has not made your

wives whom you declare unlawful your mothers. And he has not made your adopted sons your [true] sons. That is [merely] your saying by your mouths, but Allah says the truth, and He guides to the [right] way. (4) Call them by [the names of] their fathers; it is more just in the sight of Allah. But if you do not know their fathers - then they are [still] your brothers in religion and those entrusted to you. And there is no blame upon you for that in which you have erred but [only for] what your hearts intended. And ever is Allah Forgiving and Merciful. (5)

Quran 33:56-58

إِنَّ ٱللَّهَ وَمَلَـٰٓئِكَتَهُۥ يُصَلُّونَ عَلَى ٱلنَّبِىِّ يَـٰٓأَيُّهَا ٱلَّذِينَ ءَامَنُوا۟ صَلُّوا۟ عَلَيْهِ وَسَلِّمُوا۟ تَسْلِيمًا (٥٦) إِنَّ ٱلَّذِينَ يُؤْذُونَ ٱللَّهَ وَرَسُولَهُۥ لَعَنَهُمُ ٱللَّهُ فِى ٱلدُّنْيَا وَٱلْأَخِرَةِ وَأَعَدَّ لَهُمْ عَذَابًا مُّهِينًا (٥٧) وَٱلَّذِينَ يُؤْذُونَ ٱلْمُؤْمِنِينَ وَٱلْمُؤْمِنَـٰتِ بِغَيْرِ مَا ٱكْتَسَبُوا۟ فَقَدِ ٱحْتَمَلُوا۟ بُهْتَـٰنًا وَإِثْمًا مُّبِينًا (٥٨)

Indeed, Allah confers blessing upon the Prophet, and His angels [ask Him to do so]. O you who have believed, ask [Allah to confer] blessing upon him and ask [Allah to grant him] peace. (56) Indeed, those who abuse Allah and His Messenger - Allah has cursed them in this world and the Hereafter and prepared for them a humiliating punishment. (57) And those who harm believing men and believing women for [something] other than what they have earned have certainly born upon themselves a slander and manifest sin. (58)

Quran 33:60

﴿ لَّئِن لَّمْ يَنتَهِ ٱلْمُنَٰفِقُونَ وَٱلَّذِينَ فِى قُلُوبِهِم مَّرَضٌ وَٱلْمُرْجِفُونَ فِى ٱلْمَدِينَةِ لَنُغْرِيَنَّكَ بِهِمْ ثُمَّ لَا يُجَاوِرُونَكَ فِيهَآ إِلَّا قَلِيلًا ﴿٦٠﴾

If the hypocrites and those in whose hearts is disease and those who spread rumors in al-Madinah do not cease, We will surely incite

you against them; then they will not remain
your neighbors therein except for a little.
(60)

Quran 33:69-70

يَـٰٓأَيُّهَا ٱلَّذِينَ ءَامَنُوا۟ لَا تَكُونُوا۟ كَٱلَّذِينَ ءَاذَوْا۟ مُوسَىٰ فَبَرَّأَهُ ٱللَّهُ
مِمَّا قَالُوا۟ وَكَانَ عِندَ ٱللَّهِ وَجِيهًا (٦٩) يَـٰٓأَيُّهَا ٱلَّذِينَ ءَامَنُوا۟
ٱتَّقُوا۟ ٱللَّهَ وَقُولُوا۟ قَوْلًا سَدِيدًا (٧٠)

*O you who have believed, be not like those
who abused Moses; then Allah cleared him
of what they said. And he, in the sight of
Allah, was distinguished. (69) O you who
have believed, fear Allah and speak words of
appropriate justice. (70)*

Quran 39:3

أَلَا لِلَّهِ ٱلدِّينُ ٱلْخَالِصُ وَٱلَّذِينَ ٱتَّخَذُوا۟ مِن دُونِهِۦٓ أَوْلِيَآءَ مَا
نَعْبُدُهُمْ إِلَّا لِيُقَرِّبُونَآ إِلَى ٱللَّهِ زُلْفَىٰٓ إِنَّ ٱللَّهَ يَحْكُمُ بَيْنَهُمْ فِى مَا
هُمْ فِيهِ يَخْتَلِفُونَ إِنَّ ٱللَّهَ لَا يَهْدِى مَنْ هُوَ كَـٰذِبٌ كَفَّارٌ (٣)

*Unquestionably, for Allah is the pure
religion. And those who take protectors*

besides Him [say], "We only worship them that they may bring us nearer to Allah in position." Indeed, Allah will judge between them concerning that over which they differ. Indeed, Allah does not guide he who is a liar and [confirmed] disbeliever. (3)

Quran 40:28

وَقَالَ رَجُلٌ مُّؤْمِنٌ مِّنْ ءَالِ فِرْعَوْنَ يَكْتُمُ إِيمَـٰنَهُۥ أَتَقْتُلُونَ رَجُلاً أَن يَقُولَ رَبِّىَ ٱللَّهُ وَقَدْ جَآءَكُم بِٱلْبَيِّنَـٰتِ مِن رَّبِّكُمْ ۖ وَإِن يَكُ كَـٰذِبًا فَعَلَيْهِ كَذِبُهُۥ ۖ وَإِن يَكُ صَادِقًا يُصِبْكُم بَعْضُ ٱلَّذِى يَعِدُكُمْ ۖ إِنَّ ٱللَّهَ لَا يَهْدِى مَنْ هُوَ مُسْرِفٌ كَذَّابٌ (٢٨)

And a believing man from the family of Pharaoh who concealed his faith said, "Do you kill a man [merely] because he says, 'My Lord is Allah' while he has brought you clear proofs from your Lord? And if he should be lying, then upon him is [the consequence of] his lie; but if he should be truthful, there will strike you some of what *he promises you. Indeed, Allah does not guide one who is a transgressor and a liar.*

Quran 42:24

أَمْ يَقُولُونَ ٱفْتَرَىٰ عَلَى ٱللَّهِ كَذِبًا ۖ فَإِن يَشَإِ ٱللَّهُ يَخْتِمْ عَلَىٰ قَلْبِكَ ۗ وَيَمْحُ ٱللَّهُ ٱلْبَٰطِلَ وَيُحِقُّ ٱلْحَقَّ بِكَلِمَٰتِهِ ۚ إِنَّهُ عَلِيمٌۢ بِذَاتِ ٱلصُّدُورِ (٢٤)

Or do they say, "He has invented about Allah a lie"? But if Allah willed, He could seal over your heart. And Allah eliminates falsehood and establishes the truth by His words. Indeed, He is Knowing of that within the breasts. (24)

Quran 43:19-25

وَجَعَلُوا ٱلْمَلَٰئِكَةَ ٱلَّذِينَ هُمْ عِبَٰدُ ٱلرَّحْمَٰنِ إِنَٰثًا ۚ أَشَهِدُوا۟ خَلْقَهُمْ ۚ سَتُكْتَبُ شَهَٰدَتُهُمْ وَيُسْـَٔلُونَ (١٩) وَقَالُوا۟ لَوْ شَآءَ ٱلرَّحْمَٰنُ مَا عَبَدْنَٰهُم ۗ مَّا لَهُم بِذَٰلِكَ مِنْ عِلْمٍ ۖ إِنْ هُمْ إِلَّا يَخْرُصُونَ (٢٠) أَمْ ءَاتَيْنَٰهُمْ كِتَٰبًا مِّن قَبْلِهِۦ فَهُم بِهِۦ مُسْتَمْسِكُونَ (٢١) بَلْ قَالُوٓا۟ إِنَّا وَجَدْنَآ ءَابَآءَنَا عَلَىٰٓ أُمَّةٍ وَإِنَّا عَلَىٰٓ ءَاثَٰرِهِم مُّهْتَدُونَ (٢٢) وَكَذَٰلِكَ مَآ أَرْسَلْنَا مِن قَبْلِكَ فِى قَرْيَةٍ مِّن نَّذِيرٍ إِلَّا قَالَ مُتْرَفُوهَآ إِنَّا وَجَدْنَآ ءَابَآءَنَا عَلَىٰٓ أُمَّةٍ

وَإِنَّا عَلَىٰٓ ءَاثَٰرِهِم مُّقْتَدُونَ (٢٣) ۞ قَٰلَ أَوَلَوْ جِئْتُكُم بِأَهْدَىٰ مِمَّا وَجَدتُّمْ عَلَيْهِ ءَابَآءَكُمْۖ قَالُوٓاْ إِنَّا بِمَآ أُرْسِلْتُم بِهِۦ كَٰفِرُونَ (٢٤) فَٱنتَقَمْنَا مِنْهُمْۖ فَٱنظُرْ كَيْفَ كَانَ عَٰقِبَةُ ٱلْمُكَذِّبِينَ (٢٥)

And they have made the angels, who are servants of the Most Merciful, females. Did they witness their creation? Their testimony will be recorded, and they will be questioned. (19) And they said, "If the Most Merciful had willed, we would not have worshipped them." They have of that no knowledge. They are not but falsifying. (20) Or have We given them a book before the Qur'an to which they are adhering? (21) Rather, they say, "Indeed, we found our fathers upon a religion, and we are in their footsteps [rightly] guided." (22) And similarly, We did not send before you any warner into a city except that its affluent said, "Indeed, we found our fathers upon a religion, and we are, in their footsteps, following." (23) [Each warner] said, "Even if I brought you better guidance than that [religion] upon which you found your fathers?" They said, "Indeed we, in that with which you were sent, are disbelievers." (24) So we took retribution from them; then see how was the end of the deniers. (25)

Quran 43:36-39

وَمَن يَعْشُ عَن ذِكْرِ ٱلرَّحْمَٰنِ نُقَيِّضْ لَهُۥ شَيْطَٰنًا فَهُوَ لَهُۥ قَرِينٌ (٣٦) وَإِنَّهُمْ لَيَصُدُّونَهُمْ عَنِ ٱلسَّبِيلِ وَيَحْسَبُونَ أَنَّهُم مُّهْتَدُونَ (٣٧) حَتَّىٰٓ إِذَا جَآءَنَا قَالَ يَٰلَيْتَ بَيْنِى وَبَيْنَكَ بُعْدَ ٱلْمَشْرِقَيْنِ فَبِئْسَ ٱلْقَرِينُ (٣٨) وَلَن يَنفَعَكُمُ ٱلْيَوْمَ إِذ ظَّلَمْتُمْ أَنَّكُمْ فِى ٱلْعَذَابِ مُشْتَرِكُونَ (٣٩)

And whoever is blinded from remembrance of the Most Merciful - We appoint for him a devil, and he is to him a companion.
(36) And indeed, the devils avert them from the way [of guidance] while they think that they are [rightly] guided (37) Until, when he comes to Us [at Judgement], he says [to his companion], "Oh, I wish there was

between me and you the distance between
the east and west - how wretched a
companion." (38) And never will it benefit
you that Day, when you have wronged, that
you are [all] sharing in the punishment.
(39)

Quran 43:74-86

إِنَّ ٱلْمُجْرِمِينَ فِى عَذَابِ جَهَنَّمَ خَٰلِدُونَ (٧٤) لَا يُفَتَّرُ عَنْهُمْ
وَهُمْ فِيهِ مُبْلِسُونَ (٧٥) وَمَا ظَلَمْنَٰهُمْ وَلَٰكِن كَانُوا۟ هُمُ
ٱلظَّٰلِمِينَ (٧٦) وَنَادَوْا۟ يَٰمَٰلِكُ لِيَقْضِ عَلَيْنَا رَبُّكَ قَالَ إِنَّكُم
مَّٰكِثُونَ (٧٧) لَقَدْ جِئْنَٰكُم بِٱلْحَقِّ وَلَٰكِنَّ أَكْثَرَكُمْ لِلْحَقِّ
كَٰرِهُونَ (٧٨) أَمْ أَبْرَمُوٓا۟ أَمْرًا فَإِنَّا مُبْرِمُونَ (٧٩) أَمْ
يَحْسَبُونَ أَنَّا لَا نَسْمَعُ سِرَّهُمْ وَنَجْوَٰهُم بَلَىٰ وَرُسُلُنَا لَدَيْهِمْ
يَكْتُبُونَ (٨٠) قُلْ إِن كَانَ لِلرَّحْمَٰنِ وَلَدٌ فَأَنَا۠ أَوَّلُ ٱلْعَٰبِدِينَ
(٨١) سُبْحَٰنَ رَبِّ ٱلسَّمَٰوَٰتِ وَٱلْأَرْضِ رَبِّ ٱلْعَرْشِ عَمَّا
يَصِفُونَ (٨٢) فَذَرْهُمْ يَخُوضُوا۟ وَيَلْعَبُوا۟ حَتَّىٰ يُلَٰقُوا۟ يَوْمَهُمُ
ٱلَّذِى يُوعَدُونَ (٨٣) وَهُوَ ٱلَّذِى فِى ٱلسَّمَآءِ إِلَٰهٌ وَفِى
ٱلْأَرْضِ إِلَٰهٌ وَهُوَ ٱلْحَكِيمُ ٱلْعَلِيمُ (٨٤) وَتَبَارَكَ ٱلَّذِى لَهُۥ
مُلْكُ ٱلسَّمَٰوَٰتِ وَٱلْأَرْضِ وَمَا بَيْنَهُمَا وَعِندَهُۥ عِلْمُ ٱلسَّاعَةِ
وَإِلَيْهِ تُرْجَعُونَ (٨٥) وَلَا يَمْلِكُ ٱلَّذِينَ يَدْعُونَ مِن دُونِهِ
ٱلشَّفَٰعَةَ إِلَّا مَن شَهِدَ بِٱلْحَقِّ وَهُمْ يَعْلَمُونَ (٨٦)

Indeed, the criminals will be in the punishment of Hell, abiding eternally. (74) It will not be allowed to subside for them, and they, therein, are in despair. (75) And We did not wrong them, but it was they who were the wrongdoers. (76) And they will call, "O Malik, let your Lord put an end to us!" He will say, "Indeed, you will remain." (77) We had certainly brought you the truth, but most of you, to the truth, were averse. (78) Or have they devised [some] affair? But indeed, We are devising [a plan]. (79) Or do they think that We hear not their secrets and their private conversations? Yes, [We do], and Our messengers are with them recording. (80) Say, [O Muhammad], "If the Most Merciful had a son, then I would be the first of [his] worshippers." (81) Exalted is the Lord of the heavens and the earth, Lord of the Throne, above what they describe. (82) So leave them to converse vainly and amuse themselves until they meet their Day which they are promised. (83) And it is Allah who is [the only] deity in the heaven, and on the earth [the only] deity. And He is the Wise, the Knowing. (84) And blessed is He to whom belongs the dominion of the heavens and the earth and whatever is between them and with whom is knowledge of the Hour and to whom you will be returned. (85) And those they invoke besides Him do not possess [power of] intercession; but only those who testify to the truth [can benefit], and they know. (86)

Quran 45:6-11

تِلْكَ ءَايَـٰتُ ٱللَّهِ نَتْلُوهَا عَلَيْكَ بِٱلْحَقِّ فَبِأَيِّ حَدِيثٍ بَعْدَ ٱللَّهِ وَءَايَـٰتِهِۦ يُؤْمِنُونَ (٦) وَيْلٌ لِّكُلِّ أَفَّاكٍ أَثِيمٍ (٧) يَسْمَعُ ءَايَـٰتِ ٱللَّهِ تُتْلَىٰ عَلَيْهِ ثُمَّ يُصِرُّ مُسْتَكْبِرًا كَأَن لَّمْ يَسْمَعْهَا فَبَشِّرْهُ بِعَذَابٍ أَلِيمٍ (٨) وَإِذَا عَلِمَ مِنْ ءَايَـٰتِنَا شَيْـًٔا ٱتَّخَذَهَا هُزُوًا أُوْلَـٰئِكَ لَهُمْ عَذَابٌ مُّهِينٌ (٩) مِّن وَرَآئِهِمْ جَهَنَّمُ وَلَا يُغْنِى عَنْهُم مَّا كَسَبُواْ شَيْـًٔا وَلَا مَا ٱتَّخَذُواْ مِن دُونِ ٱللَّهِ أَوْلِيَآءَ وَلَهُمْ

عَذَابٌ عَظِيمٌ (١٠) هَٰذَا هُدًى ۖ وَٱلَّذِينَ كَفَرُواْ بِـَٔايَٰتِ رَبِّهِمْ لَهُمْ عَذَابٌ مِّن رِّجْزٍ أَلِيمٌ (١١)

These are the verses of Allah which We recite to you in truth. Then in what statement after Allah and His verses will they believe? (6) Woe to every sinful liar (7) Who hears the verses of Allah recited to him, then persists arrogantly as if he had not heard them. So give him tidings of a painful punishment. (8) And when he knows anything of Our verses, he takes them in ridicule. Those will have a humiliating punishment. (9) Before them is Hell, and what they had earned will not avail them at all nor what they had taken besides Allah as allies. And they will have a great punishment. (10) This [Qur'an] is guidance. And those who have disbelieved in the verses of their Lord will have a painful punishment of foul nature. (11)

Quran 47:1-3

ٱلَّذِينَ كَفَرُواْ وَصَدُّواْ عَن سَبِيلِ ٱللَّهِ أَضَلَّ أَعْمَـٰلَهُمْ
(١) وَٱلَّذِينَ ءَامَنُواْ وَعَمِلُواْ ٱلصَّـٰلِحَـٰتِ وَءَامَنُواْ بِمَا نُزِّلَ
عَلَىٰ مُحَمَّدٍ وَهُوَ ٱلْحَقُّ مِن رَّبِّهِمْ كَفَّرَ عَنْهُمْ سَيِّئَاتِهِمْ وَأَصْلَحَ
بَالَهُمْ (٢) ذَٰلِكَ بِأَنَّ ٱلَّذِينَ كَفَرُواْ ٱتَّبَعُواْ ٱلْبَـٰطِلَ وَأَنَّ ٱلَّذِينَ
ءَامَنُواْ ٱتَّبَعُواْ ٱلْحَقَّ مِن رَّبِّهِمْ كَذَٰلِكَ يَضْرِبُ ٱللَّهُ لِلنَّاسِ
أَمْثَـٰلَهُمْ (٣)

*Those who disbelieve and avert [people] from
the way of Allah - He will waste their deeds.
(1) And those who believe and do righteous
deeds and believe in what has been sent
down upon Muhammad - and it is the truth
from their Lord - He will remove from them
their misdeeds and amend their condition.
(2) That is because those who disbelieve
follow falsehood, and those who believe
follow the truth from their Lord. Thus does
Allah present to the people their
comparisons. (3)*

Quran 51:5-11

إِنَّمَا تُوعَدُونَ لَصَادِقٌ (٥) وَإِنَّ ٱلدِّينَ لَوَٰقِعٌ (٦) وَٱلسَّمَآءِ
ذَاتِ ٱلْحُبُكِ (٧) إِنَّكُمْ لَفِى قَوْلٍ مُّخْتَلِفٍ (٨) يُؤْفَكُ عَنْهُ مَنْ

أُفِكَ (٩) قُتِلَ ٱلْخَرَّاصُونَ (١٠) ٱلَّذِينَ هُمْ فِى غَمْرَةٍ سَاهُونَ (١١)

Indeed, what you are promised is true.
(5) And indeed, the recompense is to occur.
(6) By the heaven containing pathways,
(7) Indeed, you are in differing speech.
(8) Deluded away from the Qur'an is he who is deluded. (9) Destroyed are the falsifiers (10) Who are within a flood [of confusion] and heedless. (11)

Quran 58:14-22

۞ أَلَمْ تَرَ إِلَى ٱلَّذِينَ تَوَلَّوْا۟ قَوْمًا غَضِبَ ٱللَّهُ عَلَيْهِم مَّا هُم مِّنكُمْ وَلَا مِنْهُمْ وَيَحْلِفُونَ عَلَى ٱلْكَذِبِ وَهُمْ يَعْلَمُونَ (١٤) أَعَدَّ ٱللَّهُ لَهُمْ عَذَابًا شَدِيدًا إِنَّهُمْ سَآءَ مَا كَانُوا۟ يَعْمَلُونَ (١٥) ٱتَّخَذُوٓا۟ أَيْمَٰنَهُمْ جُنَّةً فَصَدُّوا۟ عَن سَبِيلِ ٱللَّهِ فَلَهُمْ عَذَابٌ مُّهِينٌ (١٦) لَّن تُغْنِىَ عَنْهُمْ أَمْوَٰلُهُمْ وَلَآ أَوْلَٰدُهُم مِّنَ ٱللَّهِ شَيْـًٔا أُو۟لَٰٓئِكَ أَصْحَٰبُ ٱلنَّارِ هُمْ فِيهَا خَٰلِدُونَ (١٧) يَوْمَ يَبْعَثُهُمُ ٱللَّهُ جَمِيعًا فَيَحْلِفُونَ لَهُۥ كَمَا يَحْلِفُونَ لَكُمْ وَيَحْسَبُونَ أَنَّهُمْ عَلَىٰ شَىْءٍ أَلَآ إِنَّهُمْ هُمُ ٱلْكَٰذِبُونَ (١٨) ٱسْتَحْوَذَ عَلَيْهِمُ ٱلشَّيْطَٰنُ فَأَنسَىٰهُمْ ذِكْرَ ٱللَّهِ أُو۟لَٰٓئِكَ حِزْبُ ٱلشَّيْطَٰنِ أَلَآ إِنَّ حِزْبَ ٱلشَّيْطَٰنِ هُمُ ٱلْخَٰسِرُونَ (١٩) إِنَّ ٱلَّذِينَ يُحَآدُّونَ ٱللَّهَ

وَرَسُولَهُ ۚ أُوْلَٰٓئِكَ فِى ٱلْأَذَلِّينَ (٢٠) كَتَبَ ٱللَّهُ لَأَغْلِبَنَّ أَنَا۠ وَرُسُلِىٓ ۚ إِنَّ ٱللَّهَ قَوِىٌّ عَزِيزٌ (٢١) لَّا تَجِدُ قَوْمًا يُؤْمِنُونَ بِٱللَّهِ وَٱلْيَوْمِ ٱلْءَاخِرِ يُوَآدُّونَ مَنْ حَآدَّ ٱللَّهَ وَرَسُولَهُ ۚ وَلَوْ كَانُوٓا۟ ءَابَآءَهُمْ أَوْ أَبْنَآءَهُمْ أَوْ إِخْوَٰنَهُمْ أَوْ عَشِيرَتَهُمْ ۚ أُوْلَٰٓئِكَ كَتَبَ فِى قُلُوبِهِمُ ٱلْإِيمَٰنَ وَأَيَّدَهُم بِرُوحٍ مِّنْهُ ۖ وَيُدْخِلُهُمْ جَنَّٰتٍ تَجْرِى مِن تَحْتِهَا ٱلْأَنْهَٰرُ خَٰلِدِينَ فِيهَا ۚ رَضِىَ ٱللَّهُ عَنْهُمْ وَرَضُوا۟ عَنْهُ ۚ أُوْلَٰٓئِكَ حِزْبُ ٱللَّهِ ۚ أَلَآ إِنَّ حِزْبَ ٱللَّهِ هُمُ ٱلْمُفْلِحُونَ (٢٢)

Have you not considered those who make allies of a people with whom Allah has become angry? They are neither of you nor of them, and they swear to untruth while they know [they are lying]. (14) Allah has prepared for them a severe punishment. Indeed, it was evil that they were doing. (15) They took their [false] oaths as a cover, so they averted [people] from the way of Allah, and for them is a humiliating punishment. (16) Never will their wealth or their children avail them against Allah at all. Those are the companions of the Fire; they will abide therein eternally (17) On the

Day Allah will resurrect them all, and they will swear to Him as they swear to you and think that they are [standing] on something. Unquestionably, it is they who are the liars. (18) Satan has overcome them and made them forget the remembrance of Allah. Those are the party of Satan. Unquestionably, the party of Satan - they will be the losers. (19) Indeed, the ones who oppose Allah and His Messenger - those will be among the most humbled. (20) Allah has written, "I will surely overcome, I and My messengers." Indeed, Allah is Powerful and Exalted in Might. (21) You will not find a people who believe in Allah and the Last Day having affection for those who oppose Allah and His Messenger, even if they were their fathers or their sons or their brothers or their kindred. Those - He has decreed within their hearts faith and supported them with spirit from Him. And We will admit them to gardens beneath which rivers flow, wherein they abide eternally. Allah is pleased with them, and they are pleased with Him - those are the party of Allah. Unquestionably, the party of Allah - they are the successful. (22)

Quran 59:11

۞ أَلَمْ تَرَ إِلَى ٱلَّذِينَ نَافَقُوا۟ يَقُولُونَ لِإِخْوَٰنِهِمُ ٱلَّذِينَ كَفَرُوا۟ مِنْ أَهْلِ ٱلْكِتَٰبِ لَئِنْ أُخْرِجْتُمْ لَنَخْرُجَنَّ مَعَكُمْ وَلَا نُطِيعُ فِيكُمْ أَحَدًا أَبَدًا وَإِن قُوتِلْتُمْ لَنَنصُرَنَّكُمْ وَٱللَّهُ يَشْهَدُ إِنَّهُمْ لَكَٰذِبُونَ (١١)

Have you not considered those who practice hypocrisy, saying to their brothers who have disbelieved among the People of the Scripture, "If you are expelled, we will surely leave with you, and we will not obey, in regard to you, anyone - ever; and if you are fought, we will surely aid you." But Allah testifies that they are liars. (11)

Quran 60:12

يَٰٓأَيُّهَا ٱلنَّبِىُّ إِذَا جَآءَكَ ٱلْمُؤْمِنَٰتُ يُبَايِعْنَكَ عَلَىٰٓ أَن لَّا يُشْرِكْنَ بِٱللَّهِ شَيْـًٔا وَلَا يَسْرِقْنَ وَلَا يَزْنِينَ وَلَا يَقْتُلْنَ أَوْلَٰدَهُنَّ وَلَا

يَأْتِينَ بِبُهْتَـٰنٍ يَفْتَرِينَهُ ۥ بَيْنَ أَيْدِيهِنَّ وَأَرْجُلِهِنَّ وَلَا يَعْصِينَكَ فِى مَعْرُوفٍ فَبَايِعْهُنَّ وَٱسْتَغْفِرْ لَهُنَّ ٱللَّهَ إِنَّ ٱللَّهَ غَفُورٌ رَّحِيمٌ (١٢)

O Prophet, when the believing women come to you pledging to you that they will not associate anything with Allah, nor will they steal, nor will they commit unlawful sexual intercourse, nor will they kill their children, nor will they bring forth a slander they have invented between their arms and legs, nor will they disobey you in what is right - then accept their pledge and ask forgiveness for them of Allah. Indeed, Allah is Forgiving and Merciful. (12)

Quran 61:6-9

وَإِذْ قَالَ عِيسَى ٱبْنُ مَرْيَمَ يَـٰبَنِىٓ إِسْرَٰٓءِيلَ إِنِّى رَسُولُ ٱللَّهِ إِلَيْكُم مُّصَدِّقًا لِّمَا بَيْنَ يَدَىَّ مِنَ ٱلتَّوْرَىٰةِ وَمُبَشِّرًۢا بِرَسُولٍ يَأْتِى مِنۢ بَعْدِى ٱسْمُهُ ۥٓ أَحْمَدُ فَلَمَّا جَآءَهُم بِٱلْبَيِّنَـٰتِ قَالُوا۟ هَـٰذَا سِحْرٌ مُّبِينٌ (٦) وَمَنْ أَظْلَمُ مِمَّنِ ٱفْتَرَىٰ عَلَى ٱللَّهِ ٱلْكَذِبَ وَهُوَ يُدْعَىٰٓ إِلَى ٱلْإِسْلَـٰمِ وَٱللَّهُ لَا يَهْدِى ٱلْقَوْمَ ٱلظَّـٰلِمِينَ (٧) يُرِيدُونَ لِيُطْفِـُٔوا۟ نُورَ ٱللَّهِ بِأَفْوَٰهِهِمْ وَٱللَّهُ مُتِمُّ نُورِهِ ۦ وَلَوْ

كَرِهَ ٱلْكَٰفِرُونَ (٨) هُوَ ٱلَّذِىٓ أَرْسَلَ رَسُولَهُۥ بِٱلْهُدَىٰ وَدِينِ ٱلْحَقِّ لِيُظْهِرَهُۥ عَلَى ٱلدِّينِ كُلِّهِۦ وَلَوْ كَرِهَ ٱلْمُشْرِكُونَ (٩)

And [mention] when Jesus, the son of Mary, said, "O children of Israel, indeed I am the messenger of Allah to you confirming what came before me of the Torah and bringing good tidings of a messenger to come after me, whose name is Ahmad." But when he came to them with clear evidences, they said, "This is obvious magic." (6) And who is more unjust than one who invents about Allah untruth while he is being invited to Islam. And Allah does not guide the wrongdoing people. (7) They want to extinguish the light of Allah with their mouths, but Allah will perfect His light, although the disbelievers dislike it. (8) It is He who sent His Messenger with guidance and the religion of truth to manifest it over all religion, although those who associate others with Allah dislike it. (9)

Quran 63:1-6

إِذَا جَاءَكَ ٱلْمُنَٰفِقُونَ قَالُوا۟ نَشْهَدُ إِنَّكَ لَرَسُولُ ٱللَّهِ ۗ وَٱللَّهُ يَعْلَمُ إِنَّكَ لَرَسُولُهُ ۥ وَٱللَّهُ يَشْهَدُ إِنَّ ٱلْمُنَٰفِقِينَ لَكَٰذِبُونَ (١) ٱتَّخَذُوٓا۟ أَيْمَٰنَهُمْ جُنَّةً فَصَدُّوا۟ عَن سَبِيلِ ٱللَّهِ ۚ إِنَّهُمْ سَآءَ مَا كَانُوا۟ يَعْمَلُونَ (٢) ذَٰلِكَ بِأَنَّهُمْ ءَامَنُوا۟ ثُمَّ كَفَرُوا۟ فَطُبِعَ عَلَىٰ قُلُوبِهِمْ فَهُمْ لَا يَفْقَهُونَ (٣) ۞ وَإِذَا رَأَيْتَهُمْ تُعْجِبُكَ أَجْسَامُهُمْ ۖ وَإِن يَقُولُوا۟ تَسْمَعْ لِقَوْلِهِمْ ۖ كَأَنَّهُمْ خُشُبٌ مُّسَنَّدَةٌ ۖ يَحْسَبُونَ كُلَّ صَيْحَةٍ عَلَيْهِمْ ۚ هُمُ ٱلْعَدُوُّ فَٱحْذَرْهُمْ ۚ قَٰتَلَهُمُ ٱللَّهُ ۖ أَنَّىٰ يُؤْفَكُونَ (٤) وَإِذَا قِيلَ لَهُمْ تَعَالَوْا۟ يَسْتَغْفِرْ لَكُمْ رَسُولُ ٱللَّهِ لَوَّوْا۟ رُءُوسَهُمْ وَرَأَيْتَهُمْ يَصُدُّونَ وَهُم مُّسْتَكْبِرُونَ (٥) سَوَآءٌ عَلَيْهِمْ أَسْتَغْفَرْتَ لَهُمْ أَمْ لَمْ تَسْتَغْفِرْ لَهُمْ لَن يَغْفِرَ ٱللَّهُ لَهُمْ ۚ إِنَّ ٱللَّهَ لَا يَهْدِى ٱلْقَوْمَ ٱلْفَٰسِقِينَ (٦)

When the hypocrites come to you, [O Muhammad], they say, "We testify that you are the Messenger of Allah." And Allah knows that you are His Messenger, and Allah testifies that the hypocrites are liars. (1) They have taken their oaths as a cover, so they averted [people] from the way of Allah. Indeed, it was evil that they were doing. (2) That is because they believed, and then they disbelieved; so their hearts were sealed over, and they do not understand. (3) And when you see them, their forms please you, and if they speak, you listen to their speech. [They are] as if they were pieces of wood propped up - they think that every shout is against them. They are the enemy, so beware of them. May Allah destroy them; how are they deluded? (4) And when it is said to them, "Come, the Messenger of Allah will ask forgiveness for you," they turn their heads aside and you see them evading while they are arrogant. (5) It is all the same for them whether you ask forgiveness for them or do not ask forgiveness for them; never will Allah forgive them. Indeed, Allah does not guide the defiantly disobedient people. (6)

Quran 68:10-13

وَلَا تُطِعْ كُلَّ حَلَّافٍ مَّهِينٍ (١٠) هَمَّازٍ مَّشَّآءٍ بِنَمِيمٍ (١١) مَّنَّاعٍ لِّلْخَيْرِ مُعْتَدٍ أَثِيمٍ (١٢) عُتُلٍّ بَعْدَ ذَٰلِكَ زَنِيمٍ (١٣)

And do not obey every worthless habitual swearer (10) [And] scorner, going about with malicious gossip - (11) A preventer of good, transgressing and sinful, (12) Cruel, moreover, and an illegitimate pretender. (13)

Quran 103

وَالْعَصْرِ (١) إِنَّ الْإِنسَٰنَ لَفِى خُسْرٍ (٢) إِلَّا الَّذِينَ ءَامَنُوا وَعَمِلُوا الصَّٰلِحَٰتِ وَتَوَاصَوْا بِالْحَقِّ وَتَوَاصَوْا بِالصَّبْرِ (٣)

By time, (1) Indeed, mankind is in loss, (2) Except for those who have believed and done righteous deeds and advised each other to truth and advised each other to patience. (3)

Quran 104

وَيْلٌ لِّكُلِّ هُمَزَةٍ لُّمَزَةٍ (١) ٱلَّذِى جَمَعَ مَالًا وَعَدَّدَهُ (٢) يَحْسَبُ أَنَّ مَالَهُ أَخْلَدَهُ (٣) كَلَّا لَيُنۢبَذَنَّ فِى ٱلْحُطَمَةِ (٤) وَمَآ أَدْرَىٰكَ مَا ٱلْحُطَمَةُ (٥) نَارُ ٱللَّهِ ٱلْمُوقَدَةُ (٦) ٱلَّتِى تَطَّلِعُ عَلَى ٱلْأَفْـِٔدَةِ (٧) إِنَّهَا عَلَيْهِم مُّؤْصَدَةٌ (٨) فِى عَمَدٍ مُّمَدَّدَةٍ (٩)

Woe to every slanderer and backbiter. (1) Who has gathered wealth and counted it, (2) He thinks that his wealth will make him last forever! (3) Nay! Verily, he will be thrown into the crushing Fire (4) And what will make you know what the crushing Fire is? (5) The fire of Allâh, kindled, (6) Which leaps up over the hearts, (7) Verily, it shall be closed upon them, (8) In pillars stretched forth (i.e. they will be punished in the Fire with pillars). (9)

Quran 114

قُلْ أَعُوذُ بِرَبِّ ٱلنَّاسِ (١) مَلِكِ ٱلنَّاسِ (٢) إِلَٰهِ ٱلنَّاسِ (٣) مِن شَرِّ ٱلْوَسْوَاسِ ٱلْخَنَّاسِ (٤) ٱلَّذِى يُوَسْوِسُ فِى صُدُورِ ٱلنَّاسِ (٥) مِنَ ٱلْجِنَّةِ وَٱلنَّاسِ (٦)

Say, "I seek refuge in the Lord of mankind,
(1) The Sovereign of mankind. (2) The God
of mankind, (3) From the evil of the
retreating whisperer - (4) Who whispers
[evil] into the breasts of mankind - (5) From
among the jinn and mankind." (6)

HADITH FORBIDDING LIES

Narrated Al-Mughirah bin Shu'bah:

that the Prophet (ﷺ) said: "Whoever narrates a Hadith from me which he knows is a lie, then he is one of the liars."

Source: Jami Tirmidhi 2662 Grade: Sahih

Narrated Ali:

The Prophet (ﷺ) said, "Do not tell a lie against me for whoever tells a lie against me then he will surely enter the Hell-fire."

Source: Sahih Bukhari 106

Ubayd Allah bin Mu'ādh al-Anbarī narrated to us, my father narrated to us; and Muhammad bin ul-Muthannā narrated to us, Abd ur-Rahman bin Mahdī both narrated to us:

Shu'bah narrated to us, on authority of Khubayb bin Abd ir-Rahman, on authority of Hafs bin Āsim, on authority of Abu Hurairah, he said, the Messenger of Allah, said:

'It is enough of a lie for a man to narrate everything he hears'.

Source: Sahih Muslim Introduction #6

It was narrated from 'Ali that:

The Prophet (ﷺ) said: '"Whoever narrates a Hadith from me thinking it to be false, then he is one of the two liars." (Either the one who invents a lie or the one who repeats it; both are liars).

Source: Sunan Ibn Majah 38 Grade: Sahih

Abdullah bin Masood reported that Muhammad (ﷺ) said:

"Should I inform you that slandering, that is in fact a tale-carrying which creates dissension amongst people, (and) he (further) said: The person tells the truth until he is recorded as truthful, and a liar tells a lie until he is recorded as a liar."

Source: Sahih Muslim 2606

Harmalah bin Yahyā bin Abd Allah bin Harmalah bin Imrān at-Tujībī narrated to me, he said Ibn Wahb narrated to us, he said Abū Shurayh narrated to me that he heard Sharāhīl bin Yazīd saying 'Muslim bin Yasar informed me that he heard Abu Hurairah saying, the Messenger of Allah said:

'There will be in the end of time charlatan liars coming to you with narrations that you nor your fathers heard, so beware of them

lest they misguide you and cause you tribulations'.'

Source: Sahih Muslim Introduction #15

Abū Sa'īd al-Ashajj narrated to me, Wakī' narrated to us, al-A'mash narrated to us, on authority of al-Musayyab bin Rāfi', on authority of Āmir bin Abdah, he said, Abd Allah bin Masood said:

'Indeed Satan will appear in the form of a man and he will come to the people, narrating to them false Ḥadīth, and they will then depart. Then a man among them will say: 'I heard a man whose face I recognize but I do not know his name narrating [such and such]...'

Source: Sahih Muslim Introduction #16

Abdullah reported Allah's Messenger (ﷺ) as saying:

"It is obligatory for you to tell the truth, for truth leads to virtue and virtue leads to Paradise, and the man who continues to speak the truth and endeavors to tell the truth is eventually recorded as truthful with Allah, and beware of telling of a lie for telling of a lie leads to obscenity and obscenity leads to Hell-Fire, and the person who keeps telling lies and endeavors to tell a lie is recorded as a liar with Allah."

Source: Sahih Muslim 2607c

Narrated Abu Huraira:

The Prophet (ﷺ) said, "He who says that I am better than Jonah bin Matta, tells a lie.'

Source: Sahih Bukhari 4805

Narrated Ibn `Umar:

Allah's Messenger (ﷺ) said, "The worst lie is that a person claims to have seen a dream which he has not seen."

Source: Sahih Bukhari 7043

Narrated Thabit bin Ad-Dahhak:

Allah's Messenger (ﷺ) said, "Whoever swears by a religion other than Islam (i.e. if somebody swears by saying that he is a non-Muslim e.g., a Jew or a Christian, etc.) in case he is telling a lie, he is really so if his oath is false, and a person is not bound to fulfill a vow about a thing which he does not possess. And if somebody commits suicide with anything in this world, he will be tortured with that very thing on the Day of Resurrection; And if somebody curses a believer, then his sin will be as if he murdered him; And whoever accuses a believer of Kufr (disbelief), then it is as if he killed him."

Source: Sahih Bukhari 6047

Narrated Abu Huraira:

The Prophet (ﷺ) said, "The signs of a hypocrite are three: Whenever he speaks he tells a lie; whenever he is entrusted he proves dishonest; whenever he promises he breaks his promise."

Source: Sahih Bukhari 2749

Aishah narrated:

"There was no behavior more hated to the Messenger of Allah than lying. A man would lie in narrating something in the presence of the Prophet, and he would not be content until he knew that he had repented."

Source: Jami Tirmidhi 1973 Grade: Hasan

Abu Hurairah narrated that the Messenger of Allah said:

"The Muslim is the brother to the Muslim, he does not cheat him, lie to him, nor deceive him. All of the Muslim is unlawful to *another Muslim: His Honor, his wealth, and his blood. At-taqwa is here. It is enough evil for a man that he belittle his brother Muslim."*

Source: Jami Tirmidhi 1927 Grade: Hasan

Narrated Abu Huraira:

When Khaibar was conquered, a roasted poisoned sheep was presented to the Prophet (ﷺ) as a gift (by the Jews). The Prophet (ﷺ) ordered, "Let all the Jews who have been here, be assembled before me." The Jews were collected and the Prophet (ﷺ) said (to them), "I am going to ask you a question. Will you tell the truth?" They said, "Yes." The Prophet (ﷺ) asked, "Who is your father?" They replied, "So-and-so." He said, "You have told a lie; your father is so-and-so." They said, "You are right." He said, "Will you now tell me the truth, if I ask you about something?" They replied, "Yes, O Abu Al-Qasim; and if we should tell a lie, you can realize our lie as you have done regarding our father." On that he asked, "Who are the people of the (Hell) Fire?" They said, "We shall remain in the (Hell) Fire for a short period, and after that you will replace us." The Prophet (ﷺ) said, "You may be cursed and humiliated in it! By Allah, we shall never replace you in it." Then he asked, "Will you now tell me the truth if I ask you a question?" They said, "Yes, O Abu Al-Qasim." He asked, "Have you poisoned this sheep?" They said, "Yes." He asked, "What made you do so?" They said, "We wanted to know if you were a liar in which case we would get rid of you, and if you are a prophet then the poison would not harm you."

Source: Sahih Bukhari 3169

Hakim bin Hazim reported Allah's Messenger (ﷺ) as saying:

"Both parties in a business transaction have the right to annul it so long as they have not separated; and if they speak the truth and make everything clear they will be blessed in their transaction; but if they tell a lie and conceal anything the blessing on their transaction will be blotted out."

Source: Sahih Muslim 1532a

Asma bint Yazid narrated that the Messenger of Allah said:

"it is not lawful to lie except in three cases: Something the man tells his wife to please her, to lie during war, and to lie in order to bring peace between the people."

Source: Jami Tirmidhi 1939 Grade: Sahih

Humaid bin 'Abd al-Rahman quoted his mother as saying:

The Prophet (ﷺ) said: "He who forged in order to put things right between two persons did not lie. The version by Ahmad ibn Muhammad and Musaddad has: The liar is not the one who puts things right between people, saying what is good and increasing good."

Source: Sunan Abi Dawud 4920 Grade: Sahih

Malik related from Safwan ibn Sulaym:

A man asked the Messenger of Allah, "Can I lie to my wife, Messenger of Allah?" The Messenger of Allah, said, "There is no good in lying." The man said, "Messenger of Allah! Shall I make her a promise and tell her?" The Messenger of Allah said, "It will not be held against you."

Source: Muwatta Imam Malik

Abu Huraira reported that the Messenger of Allah said:

"Beware of suspicion. Suspicion is the worst type of lie. Do not spy. Do not fight one another. Do not try to ensnare one another (in sales). Do not envy each other. Do not hate one another. Be slaves of Allah and brothers."

Source: Adab al Mufrad 1287 Grade: Sahih

Abu Huraira reported Allah's Messenger (ﷺ) as saying:

"Avoid suspicion, for suspicion is the gravest lie in talk and do not be inquisitive about one another and do not spy upon one another and do not feel envy with the other, and nurse no malice, and nurse no aversion and hostility against one another. And be fellow-brothers and servants of Allah."

Source: Sahih Muslim 2563a

Abdullah bin 'Amr bin Al-'As said:

The Prophet (ﷺ) said, "Whosoever possesses these four characteristics, is a sheer hypocrite; and anyone who possesses one of them, possesses a characteristic of hypocrisy till he gives it up. (These are:) When he is entrusted with something, he proves dishonest; when he talks, he tells a lie; when he makes a covenant, he acts treacherously; and when he quarrels, he utters foul language."

Source: Riyad As-Saliheen 1543 Grade: Sahih

Narrated Abdullah ibn Amir:

My mother called me one day when the Messenger of Allah (ﷺ) was sitting in our house. She said: Come here and I shall give you something. The Messenger of Allah (ﷺ)

asked her: What did you intend to give him? She replied: I intended to give him some dates. The Messenger of Allah (ﷺ) said: If you were not to give him anything, a lie would be recorded against you.

Source: Sunan Abu Dawood 4991
Grade: Hasan

Narrated `Aisha:

Two old ladies from among the Jewish ladies entered upon me and said' "The dead are punished in their graves," but I thought they were telling a lie and did not believe them in the beginning. When they went away and the Prophet (ﷺ) entered upon me, I said, "O Allah's Messenger (ﷺ)! Two old ladies.." and told him the whole story. He said, "They told the truth; the dead are really punished, to the extent that all the animals hear (the sound resulting from) their punishment." Since then I always saw him seeking refuge with Allah from the punishment of the grave in his prayers.

Source: Sahih Bukhari 6366

Umar bin Al-Khattab that the Messenger of Allah said:

"The deceased is punished for the crying of his family over him."

Source: Jami Tirmidhi 1002 Grade: Sahih

Musa bin Abi Musa Al-Asha'ri narrated from his father that:

The Messenger of Allah said: "No one dies and they stand over him crying and saying: 'O what a great man he was! O how respectful he was!' except that two angels are appointed for him to poke him (saying): 'Is that (really the reality about) you?'"

Source: Jami Tirmidhi 1003 Grade: Sahih

Narrated Al-Bara' ibn Azib:

We went out with the Messenger of Allah (ﷺ) accompanying the bier of a man of the Ansar. When we reached his grave, it was not yet dug. So the Messenger of Allah (ﷺ) sat down and we also sat down around him as if birds were over our heads. He had in his hand a stick with which he was scratching the ground.

He then raised his head and said: Seek refuge with Allah from the punishment in the grave. He said it twice or thrice.

The version of Jabir adds here: He hears the beat of their sandals when they go back, and at that moment he is asked: O so and so! Who is your Lord, what is your religion, and who is your Prophet?

Hannad's version says: Two angels will come to him, make him sit up and ask him: Who is your Lord?

He will reply: My Lord is Allah. They will ask him: What is your religion? He will reply: My religion is Islam. They will ask him: What is your opinion about the man who was sent on a mission among you? He will reply: He is the Messenger of Allah (ﷺ).

They will ask: Who made you aware of this? He will reply: I read Allah's Book, believed in it, and considered it true; which is verified by Allah's words: "Allah establishes those who believe with the word that stands firm in this world and the next."

The agreed version reads: Then a crier will call from Heaven: My servant has spoken the truth, so spread a bed for him from Paradise, clothe him from Paradise, and open a door for him into Paradise. So some of its air and perfume will come to him, and a space will be made for him as far as the eye can see.

He also mentioned the death of the infidel, saying: His spirit will be restored to his body, two angels will come to him, make him sit up and ask him: Who is your Lord? He will reply: Alas, alas! I do not know. They will ask him: What is your religion? He will reply: Alas, alas! I do not know. They will ask: Who was the man who was sent on a mission among you? He will reply: Alas, alas! I do not know. Then a crier will call from Heaven: He has lied, so spread a bed for him from Hell, clothe him from Hell, and open for him a door into Hell. Then some of its heat and pestilential wind will come to him, and his grave will be compressed, so that his ribs will be crushed together.

Jabir's version adds: One who is blind and dumb will then be placed in charge of him, having a sledge-hammer such that if a mountain were struck with it, it would become dust. He will give him a blow with it which will be heard by everything between the east and the west except by men and jinn, and he will become dust. Then his spirit will be restored to him (for further punishment).

Source: Sunan Abu Dawood 4753
Grade: Sahih

Narrated Samura bin Jundab:

Whenever the Prophet (ﷺ) finished the (morning) prayer, he would face us and ask, "Who amongst you had a dream last night?" So if anyone had seen a dream he would narrate it. The Prophet (ﷺ) would say: "Ma sha'a-llah" (An Arabic maxim meaning literally, 'What Allah wished,' and it indicates a good omen.) One day, he asked us whether anyone of us had seen a dream. We replied in the negative. The Prophet said, "But I had seen (a dream) last night that two men came to me, caught hold of my hands, and took me to the Sacred Land (Jerusalem). There, I saw a person sitting and another standing with an iron hook in his hand pushing it inside the mouth of the former till it reached the jawbone, and then tore off one side of his cheek, and then did the same with the other side; in the meantime the first side of his cheek became normal again and then he repeated the same operation again. I said, 'What is this?' They told me to proceed on and we went on till we came to a man Lying flat on his back, and another man standing at his head carrying a stone or a piece of rock, and crushing the head of the Lying man, with that stone. Whenever he struck him, the stone rolled away. The man went to pick it up and by the time he returned to him, the crushed head had returned to its normal state and the man came back and struck him again (and so on). I said, 'Who is this?' They told me to proceed on; so we proceeded on and passed by a hole like an oven; with a narrow top and wide bottom, and the fire was kindling underneath that hole. Whenever the fire-flame went up, the people were lifted up to such an extent that they about to get out of it, and whenever the fire got quieter, the people went down into it, and there were naked men and women in it. I said, 'Who is this?' They told me to proceed on. So we proceeded on till we reached a river of blood and a man was in it, and another man was standing at its bank with stones in front of him, facing the man standing in the river. Whenever the man in the river wanted to come out, the other one threw a stone in his mouth and caused him to retreat to his original position; and so whenever he wanted to come out the other would throw a stone in his mouth, and he would retreat to his original position. I asked, 'What is this?' They told me to proceed on and we did so till we reached a well-flourished green garden having a huge tree and near its root was sitting an old man with some children. (I saw) Another man near the tree with fire in front of him and he was kindling it up. Then they (i.e. my two companions) made me climb up the tree and made me enter a house, better than which I have ever seen. In it were some old men and young men, women and children. Then they took me out of this house and made me climb up the tree and made me enter another house that was better and superior (to the first) containing old and young people. I said to them (i.e. my two companions), 'You have made me ramble all the night. Tell me all about that I have seen.' They said, 'Yes. As for the one whose cheek you saw being torn away, he was a liar and he used to tell lies, and the people would report those lies on his authority till they spread all over the world. So, he will be punished like that till the Day of Resurrection. The one whose head you *saw being crushed is the one whom Allah had given the knowledge of Qur'an (i.e. knowing it by heart) but he used to sleep at night (i.e. he did not recite it then) and did not use to act upon it (i.e. upon its orders etc.) by day; and so this punishment will go on till the Day of Resurrection. And those you saw in the hole (like oven) were adulterers (those men and women who commit illegal sexual intercourse). And those you saw in the river of blood were those dealing in Riba (usury/interest). And the old man who was sitting at the base of the tree was Abraham and the little children around him were the offspring of the people. And the one who was kindling the fire was Malik, the gatekeeper of the Hell-fire. And the first house in which you have gone was the house of the common believers, and the second house was of the martyrs. I am Gabriel and this is Michael. Raise your head.' I raised my head and saw a thing like a cloud over me. They said, 'That is your place.' I said, 'Let me enter my place.' They said, 'You still have some life which you have not yet completed, and when you complete (that remaining portion of your life) you will then enter your place.' "*

Source: Sahih Bukhari 1386

Narrated Abu Huraira:

that he heard Allah's Messenger (ﷺ) saying, "Allah willed to test three Israelis who were a Leper, a blind man and a bald-headed man. So, he sent them an angel who came to the leper and said, 'What thing do you like most?' He replied, 'Good color and good skin, for the people have a strong aversion to me.' The angel touched him and his illness was cured, and he was given a good color and beautiful skin. The angel asked him, 'What kind of property do you like best?' He replied, 'Camels (or cows).' (The narrator is in doubt, for either the leper or the bald-headed man demanded camels and the other demanded cows). So he (i.e. the leper) was given a pregnant she-camel, and the angel said (to him), 'May Allah bless you in it.' The angel then went to the bald-headed man and said, 'What thing do you like most?' He said, 'I like good hair and wish to be cured of this disease, for the people feel repulsion for me.' The angel touched him and his illness was cured, and he was given good hair. The angel asked (him), 'What kind of property do you like best?' He replied, 'Cows,' The angel gave him a pregnant cow and said, 'May Allah bless you in it.' The angel went to the blind man and asked, 'What thing do you like best?' He said, '(I like) that Allah may restore my eye-sight to me so that I may see the people.' The angel touched his eyes and Allah gave him back his eye-sight. The angel asked him, 'What kind of property do you like best?' He replied, 'Sheep.' The angel gave him a pregnant sheep. Afterwards, all the three pregnant animals gave birth to young ones, and multiplied and brought forth so much that one of the (three) men had a herd of camels filling a valley, and one had a herd of cows filling a valley, and one had a flock of sheep filling a valley. Then the angel, disguised in the shape and appearance of a leper, went to the leper and said, I am a poor man, who has lost all means of livelihood while on a journey. So none will satisfy my need except Allah and then you. In the Name of Him Who has given you such nice color and beautiful skin, and so much property, I ask you to give me a camel so that I may reach my destination. The man replied, 'I have many obligations (so I cannot give you).' The angel said, 'I think I know you; were you not a leper to whom the people had a strong aversion? Weren't you a poor man, and then Allah gave you (all this property).' He replied, '(This is all wrong), I got this property through inheritance from my fore-fathers.' The angel said, 'If you are telling a lie, then let Allah make you as you were before.' Then the angel, disguised in the shape and appearance of a bald man, went to the bald man and said to him the same as he told the first one, and he too answered the same as the first one did. The angel said, 'If you are telling a lie, then let Allah make you as you were before.' The angel, disguised in the shape of a blind man, went to the blind man and said, 'I am a poor man and a traveler, whose means of livelihood have been exhausted while on a journey. I have nobody to help me except Allah, and after Him, you yourself. I ask you in the Name of Him Who has given you back your eye-sight to give me a sheep, so that with its help, I may complete my journey.' The man said, 'No doubt, I was blind and Allah gave me back my eye-sight; I was poor and Allah made me rich; so take anything you wish from my property. By Allah, I will not stop you for taking anything (you need) of my property which you may take for Allah's sake.' The angel replied, 'Keep your property with you. You (i.e the three men) have been tested, and Allah is pleased with you and is angry with your two companions."

Source: Sahih Bukhari 3464

Ibn 'Umar said:

Some jews came to the Messenger of Allah (ﷺ) and mentioned to him that a man and a women of their number had committed fornication. The Messenger of Allah (ﷺ) asked them: What do you find in the Torah about stoning? They replied: We disgrace them and they should be flogged. 'Abd Allah bin Salam said: You lie; it contains (instruction for) stoning. So they brought the Torah and spread it out, and one of them put his hand over the verse of stoning and read what preceded it and what followed it. 'Abd Allah bin Salam said to him: Lift your hand. When he did so, the verse of stoning was seen to be in it. They then said: He has spoken the truth, Muhammad, the verse of stoning is in it. The Messenger of Allah (ﷺ) then gave command regarding them, and they were stoned to death. 'Abd Allah bin 'Umar said: I saw the man leaning on the woman protecting her from the stones.

Source: Sunan Abi Dawud 4446 Grade: Sahih

It was narrated from Ibn 'Abbas that:

Hilal bin Umayyah accused his wife in the presence of the Prophet (ﷺ) of (committing adultery) with Sharik bin Sahma'. The Prophet said: "Bring proof or you will feel the Hadd (punishment) on your back." Hilal bin Umayyah said: "By the One Who sent

*you with the truth, I am telling the truth,
and Allah will send down revelation
concerning my situation which will spare
my back." Then the following was revealed:
"And for those who accuse their wives, but
have no witnesses except themselves, let the
testimony of one of them be four testimonies
(i.e., testifies four times) by Allah that he is
one of those who speak the truth. And the
fifth (testimony should be) the invoking of
the curse of Allah on him if he be of those
who tell a lie (against her). But it shall avert
the punishment (of stoning to death) from
her, it she bears witness four times by Allah,
that he (her husband) is telling a lie. And
the fifth (testimony) should be that the
wrath of Allah be upon her if he (her
husband) speaks the truth." The Prophet
(ﷺ), turned and sent for them, and they
came. Hilal bin Umayyah stood up and bore
witness, and the Prophet (ﷺ) said: "Allah
knows that one of you is lying. Will either of*

you repent?" Then she stood up and affirmed her innocence. On the fifth time, meaning that the wrath of Allah be upon her if he (her husband) speaks the truth, they said to her: "It will invoke the wrath of Allah." Ibn 'Abbas said: "She hesitated and backed up, until we thought that she was going to recant. Then she said: 'By Allah, I cannot dishonor my people forever.' Then the Prophet (ﷺ) said: 'Wait and see. If she gives birth to a child with black eyes, fleshy buttocks and big calves, then he is the son of Sharik bin Sahma'.' And she gave birth to such a child. Then the Prophet (ﷺ) said: 'Had it not the matter been settled by the Book of Allah, I would have punished her severely.' "

Source: Sunan Ibn Majah 2067 Grade: Sahih

Narrated Sa`id bin Jubair:

I asked Ibn `Umar, "(What is the verdict if) a man accuses his wife of illegal sexual intercourse?" Ibn `Umar said, "The Prophet (ﷺ) separated (by divorce) the couple of Bani Al-Ajlan, and said, (to them), 'Allah knows that one of you two is a liar; so will one of you repent?' But both of them refused. He again said, 'Allah knows that one of you two is a liar; so will one of you repent?' But both of them refused. So he separated them by divorce." (Aiyub, a sub-narrator said: `Amr bin Dinar said to me, "There is something else in this Hadith which you have not mentioned. It goes thus: The man said, 'What about my money (i.e. the Mahr(Dowry) that I have given to my wife)?' It was said, 'You have no right to restore any money, for if you have spoken the truth (as regards the accusation), you have also consummated your marriage with her; and if you have told a lie, you are less rightful to have your money back.' ")

Source: Sahih Bukhari 5311

Narrated Abdullah ibn Masood:

The Messenger of Allah (ﷺ) said: He who swears an oath in which he tells a lie to take the property of a Muslim by unfair means, will meet Allah while He is angry with him.

Al-Ash'ath said: I swear by Allah, he said this about me. There was some land between me and a Jew, but he denied it to me; so I presented him to the Prophet (ﷺ).

The Prophet (ﷺ) asked me: Have you any evidence? I replied: No. He said to the Jew: Take an oath. I said: Messenger of Allah, now he will take an oath and take my property. So Allah, the Exalted, revealed the verse, "As for those who sell the faith they owe to Allah and their own plighted word for a small price, they shall have no portion in the hereafter."

Source: Sunan Abi Dawud 3243 Grade: Sahih

Sa'id bin Zaid bin 'Amr bin Nufail reported that Arwi (bint Uwais) disputed with him (in regard to a part of the land) of his house. He said:

Leave it and take off your claim from it, for I heard Allah's Messenger (ﷺ) as saying: He who took a span of land without his right would be made to wear around his neck seven earths on the Day of Resurrection. He (Sa'id bin Zaid) said: O Allah, make her blind if she has told a lie and make her grave in her house. He (the narrator) said: I saw her blind groping (her way) by touching the walls and saying: The curse of Sa'id bin Zaid has hit me. And it so happened that as she was walking in her house, she passed by a well in her house and fell therein and that became her grave.

Source: Sahih Muslim 1610b

Narrated Zaid bin Arqam:

We went out with the Prophet (ﷺ): on a journey and the people suffered from lack of provisions. So `Abdullah bin Ubai said to his companions, "Don't spend on those who are with Allah's Messenger (ﷺ), that they may disperse and go away from him." He also said, "If we return to Medina, surely, the more honorable will expel therefrom the meaner." So I went to the Prophet (ﷺ) and informed him of that. He sent for `Abdullah bin Ubai and asked him, but `Abdullah bin Ubai swore that he did not say so. The people said, "Zaid told a lie to 'Allah's Messenger (ﷺ)." What they said distressed me very much. Later Allah revealed the confirmation of my statement in his saying:- - '(When the hypocrites come to you.' (63.1) So the Prophet (ﷺ) called them that they might ask Allah to forgive them, but they *turned their heads aside. (Regarding Allah's saying: 'Pieces of wood propped up,' Zaid said; They were the most handsome men.)*

Source: Sahih Bukhari 4903

Malik related from Muhammad ibn al-Munkadir that Umayma bint Ruqayqa said: *"I went to the Messenger of Allah with the women who took an oath of allegiance with him in Islam.*

They said, 'Messenger of Allah! We take a pledge with you not to associate anything with Allah, not to steal, not to commit adultery, not to kill our children, nor to produce any lie that we have devised between our hands and feet, and not to disobey you in what is known.' The Messenger of Allah said, 'In what you can do and are able.' "

Umayma continued, "They said, 'Allah and His Messenger are more merciful to us than ourselves. Come, let us give our hands to you, Messenger of Allah!'

The Messenger of Allah said, 'I do not shake hands with women. My word to a hundred women is like my word to one woman.' "

Source: Muwatta Imam Malik

Uqbah bin Suhban said:

"I heard 'Uthman bin 'Affan say: 'I never sang a song or told a lie or touched my penis with my right hand after I swore on oath of allegiance to the Messenger of Allah to that effect.'"

Source: Sunan Ibn Majah 311 Grade: Daif

Salamah bin Al-Akwa reported:

My father said that a person ate in the presence of Messenger of Allah (ﷺ) with his left hand. He (ﷺ) said, "Eat with your right hand". He said, "I cannot do that."

Thereupon he (the Prophet) said, "May you never do that." It was pride that prevented him from doing it. And he could not raise it (the right hand) up to his mouth afterwards.

Source: Riyad Salihin 159 Grade: Sahih

Narrated 'Aishah:

that a man came and sat in front of the Messenger of Allah (ﷺ) and said: "O Messenger of Allah! I have two slaves who lie to me, deceive me, and disobey me, and I scold them and hit them. So what is my case because of them?" He said: "The extent to which they betrayed you, disobeyed you and lied to you will be measured against how much you punish them. If your punishing them is equal to their sins, then the two will be the same, nothing for you and nothing against you. If your punishing them is above their sin, some of your rewards will be taken from you and given to them." So the man left, and began weeping and crying aloud. The Messenger of Allah (ﷺ) said: "You should read what Allah said in His Book: 'And We shall set up the Balances of justice on the Day of Resurrection, then none will be dealt with unjustly in anything...' to the rest of the Ayah (21:47). So the man said: "By Allah, O Messenger of Allah! I see nothing better for myself, than me parting with them. Bear witness that they are all free."

Source: Jami Tirmidhi 3165 Grade: Daif

Abu Hurairah narrated that the Messenger of Allah said:

"Do you know who the bankrupt is?" They said: "O Messenger of Allah! The bankrupt among us is the one who has no Dirham nor property." The Messenger of Allah said: "The bankrupt in my Ummah is the one who comes with Salat and fasting and Zakat

on the Day of Judgement, but he comes
having abused this one, falsely accusing that
one, wrongfully consuming the wealth of
this one, spilling the blood of that one, and
beating this one. So he is seated, and this one
is requited from his rewards. If his rewards
are exhausted before the sins that he
committed are requited, then some of their
sins will be taken and cast upon him, then
he will be cast into the Fire."

Source: Jami Tirmidhi 2418 Grade: Sahih

Abu Hurairah reported:

The Messenger of Allah (ﷺ) put me in
charge of charity of Ramadan (Sadaqat-ul-
Fitr). Somebody came to me and began to
take away some food-stuff. I caught him and
said, "I must take you to the Messenger of
Allah (ﷺ)." He said, "I am a needy man
with a large family, and so I have a pressing
need." I let him go. When I saw the

Messenger of Allah (ﷺ) next morning, he asked me, "O Abu Hurairah! What did your captive do last night?" I said, "O Messenger of Allah! He complained of a pressing need and a big family. I felt pity for him so I let him go." He (ﷺ) said, "He told you a lie and he will return."

I was sure, according to the saying of the Messenger of Allah (ﷺ) that he would return. I waited for him. He sneaked up again and began to steal food-stuff from the Sadaqah. I caught him and said; "I must take you to the Messenger of Allah (ﷺ)." He said, "Let go of me, I am a needy man. I have to bear the expenses of a big family. I will not come back." So I took pity on him and let him go. I went at dawn to the Messenger of Allah (ﷺ) who asked me, "O Abu Hurairah! What did your captive do last night?" I replied, "O Messenger of Allah! He complained of a pressing want and the burden of a big family. I took pity on him and so I let him go." He (ﷺ) said, "He told you a lie and he will return."

(That man) came again to steal the food-stuff. I arrested him and said, "I must take you to the Messenger of Allah (ﷺ), and this is the last of three times. You promised that you would not come again but you did." He said, "Let go of me, I shall teach you some words with which Allah may benefit you." I asked, "What are those words?" He replied, "When you go to bed, recite Ayat-ul- Kursi (2:255) for there will be a guardian appointed over you from Allah, and Satan will not be able to approach you till morning." So I let him go.

Next morning the Messenger of Allah (ﷺ) asked me, "What did your prisoner do last night." I answered, "He promised to teach me some words which he claimed will benefit me before Allah. So I let him go." The

Messenger of Allah (ﷺ) asked, "What are those words that he taught you?" I said, "He told me: 'When you go to bed, recite Ayat- ul-Kursi from the beginning to the end i.e.,[Allah! none has the right to be worshipped but He, the Ever Living, the One Who sustains and protects all that exists. Neither slumber nor sleep overtakes Him. To Him belongs whatever is in the heavens and whatever is on the earth. Who is he that can intercede with Him except with His Permission? He knows what happens to them (His creatures) in this world, and what will happen to them in the Hereafter. And they will never compass anything of His Knowledge except that which He wills. His Kursi encompasses the heavens and the earth, and preserving them does not fatigue Him. And He is the Most High, the Most Great].' (2:255). He added: 'By reciting it, there will be a guardian appointed over you from Allah who will *protect you during the night, and Satan will not be able to come near you until morning'." The Messenger of Allah (ﷺ) said, "Verily, he has told you the truth though he is a liar. O Abu Hurairah! Do you know with whom you were speaking for the last three nights?" I said, "No." He (ﷺ) said, "He was Satan."*

Source: Riyad As-Saliheen 1020 Grade: Sahih

Narrated `Abdullah bin Ka`b bin Malik [he was among Ka`b's sons, the guide of Ka`b when he became blind]:

I heard Ka`b bin Malik narrating the story of (the Battle of) Tabuk in which he failed to take part. Ka`b said, "I did not remain behind Allah's Messenger (ﷺ) in any Battle that he fought except the Battle of Tabuk, and I failed to take part in the Battle of Badr, but Allah did not admonish anyone who had not participated in it, for in fact, Allah's Messenger (ﷺ) had gone out in search of the caravan of Quraish till Allah made them (i.e. the Muslims) and their enemy meet without any appointment. I witnessed the night of Al-`Aqaba (pledge) with Allah's Messenger (ﷺ) when we pledged for Islam, and I would not exchange it for the Badr battle although the Badr battle is more popular amongst the people than it (i.e. Al-`Aqaba pledge).

As for my news (in this battle of Tabuk), I had never been stronger or wealthier than I was when I remained behind the Prophet (ﷺ) in that Battle. By Allah, never had I two she-camels before, but I had then at the time of this Battle. Whenever Allah's Messenger (ﷺ) wanted to make a Battle, he used to hide his intention by apparently referring to different Battle till it was the time of that Battle (of Tabuk) which Allah's Messenger (ﷺ) fought in severe heat, facing, a long *journey, desert, and the great number of enemy. So the Prophet (ﷺ) announced to the Muslims clearly (their destination) so that they might get prepared for their Battle. So he informed them clearly of the destination he was going to. Allah's Messenger (ﷺ) was accompanied by a large number of Muslims who could not be listed in a book namely, a register."*

Ka`b added, "Any man who intended to be absent would think that the matter would remain hidden unless Allah revealed it through Divine Revelation. So Allah's Messenger (ﷺ) fought that Battle at the time when the fruits had ripened and the shade looked pleasant. Allah's Messenger (ﷺ) and his companions prepared for the battle and I started to go out in order to get myself ready along with them, but I returned without doing anything. I would say to myself, 'I can do that.' So I kept on delaying it every *now and then till the people got ready and Allah's Messenger (ﷺ) and the Muslims along with him departed, and I had not prepared anything for my departure, and I said, I will prepare myself (for departure) one or two days after him, and then join them.' In the morning following their departure, I went out to get myself ready but returned having done nothing. Then again in the next morning, I went out to get ready but returned without doing anything. Such was the case with me till they hurried away and the battle was missed (by me). Even then I intended to depart to take them over. I wish I had done so! But it was not in my destiny. So, after the departure of Allah's Messenger (ﷺ), whenever I went out and walked amongst the people (i.e, the remaining persons), it grieved me that I could see none around me, but one accused of hypocrisy or one of those weak men whom Allah had excused.*

Allah's Messenger (ﷺ) did not remember me till he reached Tabuk. So while he was sitting amongst the people in Tabuk, he said, 'What did Ka`b do?' A man from Banu Salama said, 'O Allah's Messenger (ﷺ)! He has been stopped by his two Burdas (i.e. garments) and his looking at his own flanks with pride.' Then Mu`adh bin Jabal said, 'What a bad thing you have said! By Allah! O Allahs Messenger! We know nothing about him but good.' Allah's Messenger (ﷺ) kept silent." Ka`b bin Malik added, "When I heard that he (i.e. the Prophet (ﷺ)) was on his way back to Medina. I got dipped in my concern, and began to think of false excuses, saying to myself, 'How can I avoid his anger tomorrow?' And I took the advice of wise member of my family in this matter. When it was said that Allah's Messenger (ﷺ), had come near, all the evil false excuses abandoned from my mind and I knew well that I could never come out of this problem *by forging a false statement. Then I decided firmly to speak the truth.*

So Allah's Messenger (ﷺ) arrived in the morning, and whenever he returned from a journey, he used to visit the Mosque first of all and offer a two-rak`at prayer therein and then sit for the people. So when he had done all that (this time), those who had failed to join the battle (of Tabuk) came and started offering (false) excuses and taking oaths before him. They were something over eighty men; Allah's Messenger (ﷺ) accepted the excuses they had expressed, took their pledge of allegiance asked for Allah's Forgiveness for them, and left the secrets of their hearts for Allah to judge. Then I came to him, and when I greeted him, he smiled a smile of an angry person and then said, 'Come on.' So I came walking till I sat before him. He said to me, 'What stopped you from joining us. Had you not purchased an animal for carrying you?' I answered, "Yes, O Allah's Messenger (ﷺ)! But by Allah, if I were sitting before any person from among the people of the world other than you, I would have avoided his anger with an excuse. By Allah, I have been bestowed with the power of speaking fluently and eloquently, but by Allah, I knew well that if today I tell you a lie to seek your favor, Allah would surely make you angry with me in the near future, but if I tell you the truth, though you will get angry because of it, I hope for Allah's Forgiveness. Really, by Allah, there was no excuse for me. By Allah, I had never been stronger or wealthier than I was when I remained behind you.' Then Allah's Messenger (ﷺ) said, 'As regards this man, he has surely told the truth. So get up till Allah decides your case.'

I got up, and many men of Banu Salama followed me and said to me. 'By Allah, we

*never witnessed you doing any sin before
this. Surely, you failed to offer excuse to
Allah's Messenger (ﷺ) as the others who did
not join him, have offered. The prayer of
Allah's Messenger (ﷺ) to Allah to forgive
you would have been sufficient for you.' By
Allah, they continued blaming me so much
that I intended to return (to the Prophet)
and accuse myself of having told a lie, but I
said to them, 'Is there anybody else who has
met the same fate as I have?' They replied,
'Yes, there are two men who have said the
same thing as you have, and to both of them
was given the same order as given to you.' I
said, 'Who are they?' They replied, Murara
bin Ar-Rabi Al- Amri and Hilal bin Umaiya
Al-Waqifi.' By that they mentioned to me
two pious men who had attended the Battle
of Badr, and in whom there was an example
for me. So I did not change my mind when
they mentioned them to me.*

Allah's Messenger (ﷺ) forbade all the Muslims to talk to us, the three aforesaid persons out of all those who had remained behind in that Battle. So we kept away from the people and they changed their attitude towards us till the very land (where I lived in) appeared strange to me as if I did not know it. We remained in that condition for fifty nights.

As regards my two fellows, they remained in their houses and kept on weeping, but I was the youngest of them and the firmest of them, so I used to go out and witness the prayers along with the Muslims and roam about in the markets, but none would talk to me, and I would come to Allah's Messenger (ﷺ) and greet him while he was sitting In his gathering after the prayer, and I would wonder whether the Prophet (ﷺ) did move his lips in return to my greetings or not. Then I would offer my prayer near to him and look at him stealthily. When I was busy with my prayer, he would turn his face towards me, but when I turned my face to him, he would turn his face away from me. When this harsh attitude of the people lasted long, I walked till I scaled the wall of the garden of Abu Qatada who was my cousin and dearest person to me, and I offered my greetings to him. By Allah, he did not return my greetings. I said, 'O Abu Qatada! I beseech you by Allah! Do you know that I love Allah and His Messenger?' He kept quiet. I asked him again, beseeching him by Allah, but he remained silent. Then I asked him again in the Name of Allah. He said, "Allah and His Messenger know it better.' Thereupon my eyes flowed with tears and I returned and jumped over the wall."

Ka`b added, "While I was walking in the market of Medina, suddenly I saw a Nabati (i.e. a Christian farmer) from the Nabatis of

Sham who came to sell his grains in Medina, saying, 'Who will lead me to Ka`b bin Malik?' The people began to point (me) out for him till he came to me and handed me a letter from the king of Ghassan in which the following was written: "To proceed, I have been informed that your friend (i.e. the Prophet (ﷺ)) has treated you harshly. Anyhow, Allah does not let you live at a place where you feel inferior and your right is lost. So join us, and we will console you." When I read it, I said to myself, 'This is also a sort of a test.' Then I took the letter to the oven and made a fire therein by burning it.

When forty out of the fifty nights elapsed, behold ! There came to me the messenger of Allah's Messenger (ﷺ) and said, 'Allah's Messenger (ﷺ) orders you to keep away from your wife,' I said, 'Should I divorce her; or else! what should I do?' He said, 'No, only keep aloof from her and do not cohabit her.'

The Prophet (ﷺ) sent the same message to my two fellows. Then I said to my wife. 'Go to your parents and remain with them till Allah gives His Verdict in this matter." Ka`b added, "The wife of Hilal bin Umaiya came to the Prophet and said, 'O Allah's Messenger (ﷺ)! Hilal bin Umaiya is a helpless old man who has no servant to attend on him. Do you dislike that I should serve him? ' He said, 'No (you can serve him) but he should not come near you.' She said, 'By Allah, he has no desire for anything. By, Allah, he has never ceased weeping till his case began till this day of his.' On that, some of my family members said to me, 'Will you also ask Allah's Messenger (ﷺ) to permit your wife (to serve you) as he has permitted the wife of Hilal bin Umaiya to serve him?' I said, 'By Allah, I will not ask the permission of Allah's Messenger (ﷺ) regarding her, for I do not know What Allah's Messenger (ﷺ) would *say if I asked him to permit her (to serve me) while I am a young man.'*

Then I remained in that state for ten more nights after that till the period of fifty nights was completed starting from the time when Allah's Messenger (ﷺ) prohibited the people from talking to us. When I had offered the Fajr prayer on the 50th morning on the roof of one of our houses and while I was sitting in the condition which Allah described in the Qur'an (i.e. my very soul seemed straitened to me and even the earth seemed narrow to me for all its spaciousness), there I heard the voice of one who had ascended the mountain of Sala' calling with his loudest voice, 'O Ka`b bin Malik! Be happy (by receiving good tidings).' I fell down in prostration before Allah, realizing that relief has come.

Allah's Messenger (ﷺ) had announced the acceptance of our repentance by Allah when he had offered the Fajr prayer. The people

then went out to congratulate us. Some
bringers of good tidings went out to my two
fellows, and a horseman came to me in haste,
and a man of Banu Aslam came running
and ascended the mountain and his voice
was swifter than the horse. When he whose
voice I had heard, came to me conveying the
good tidings, I took off my garments and
dressed him with them; and by Allah, I
owned no other garments than them on that
day. Then I borrowed two garments and
wore them and went to Allah's Messenger.
The people started receiving me in batches,
congratulating me on Allah's Acceptance of
my repentance, saying, 'We congratulate
you on Allah's Acceptance of your
repentance." Ka`b further said, "When I
entered the Mosque. I saw Allah's
Messenger (ﷺ) sitting with the people
around him. Talha bin Ubaidullah swiftly
came to me, shook hands with me and
congratulated me. By Allah, none of the

Muhajirin (i.e. Emigrants) got up for me except him (i.e. Talha), and I will never forget this for Talha."

Ka`b added, "When I greeted Allah's Messenger he, his face being bright with joy, said "Be happy with the best day that you have got ever since your mother delivered you." Ka`b added, "I said to the Prophet (ﷺ) 'Is this forgiveness from you or from Allah?' He said, 'No, it is from Allah.' Whenever Allah's Messenger (ﷺ) became happy, his face would shine as if it were a piece of moon, and we all knew that characteristic of him. When I sat before him, I said, 'O Allah's Messenger (ﷺ)! Because of the acceptance of my repentance I will give up all my wealth as alms for the Sake of Allah and His Messenger.

Allah's Messenger said, 'Keep some of your wealth, as it will be better for you.'

I said, 'So I will keep my share from Khaibar with me,' and added, 'O Allah's Messenger (ﷺ)! Allah has saved me for telling the truth; so it is a part of my repentance not to tell but the truth as long as I am alive.

By Allah, I do not know anyone of the Muslims whom Allah has helped for telling the truth more than me. Since I have mentioned that truth to Allah's Messenger (ﷺ) till today, I have never intended to tell a lie. I hope that Allah will also save me (from telling lies) the rest of my life. So Allah revealed to His Messenger the Verse:-- "Verily, Allah has forgiven the Prophet, the Muhajirin (i.e. Emigrants) (up to His Saying) And be with those who are true (in word and deed)." (9.117-119) By Allah, Allah has never bestowed upon me, apart from His guiding me to Islam, a Greater blessing than the fact that I did not tell a lie *to Allah's Messenger (ﷺ) which would have caused me to perish as those who have told a lie perished, for Allah described those who told lies with the worst description He ever attributed to anybody else.*

Allah said:-- "They (i.e. the hypocrites) will swear by Allah to you when you return to them (up to His Saying) Certainly Allah is not pleased with the rebellious people-- " (9.95-96)

Ka`b added, "We, the three persons, differed altogether from those whose excuses Allah's Messenger accepted when they swore to him. He took their pledge of allegiance and asked Allah to forgive them, but Allah's Messenger (ﷺ) left our case pending till Allah gave His Judgment about it. As for that Allah said:-- And to the three (He did forgive also) who remained behind." (9.118) What Allah said (in this Verse) does not indicate our failure to take part in the Battle, *but it refers to the deferment of making a decision by the Prophet (ﷺ) about our case in contrast to the case of those who had taken an oath before him and he excused them by accepting their excuses.*

Source: Sahih Bukhari 4418

It was narrated from Abu Hurairah that the Messenger of Allah (ﷺ) said:

"There will come to the people years of treachery, when the liar will be regarded as honest, and the honest man will be regarded as a liar; the traitor will be regarded as faithful, and the faithful man will be regarded as a traitor; and the Ruwaibidah will decide matters.' It was said: 'Who are the Ruwaibidah?' He said: 'Vile and base men who control the affairs of the people.'"

Source: Sunan Ibn Majah 4036 Grade: Hasan

Abu Huraira reported Allah's Messenger (ﷺ) as saying:

"The Last Hour would not come until there would arise about thirty impostors, liars, and each one of them would claim that he is a messenger of Allah"

Source: Sahih Muslim 157 m

It was narrated that Anas said:

"The Messenger of Allah said: 'There was no Prophet except that he warned his Ummah of the liar who is blind in one eye. (The Dajjal/Antichrist) Lo! He is blind in one eye, and your Lord is not blind in one eye. Written between his eyes is: Kafir(disbeliever).'"

Source: Jami Tirmidhi 2245 Grade: Sahih

Malik related to me that Safwan ibn Sulaym said:

"The Messenger of Allah was asked, 'Can the believer be a coward?' He said, 'Yes.' He was asked, 'Can the believer be a miser?' He said, 'Yes.' He was asked, 'Can the believer be a liar?' He said, 'No.' "

Source: Muwatta Imam Malik

Abu Hurairah said:

The Messenger of Allah (ﷺ) said, "There are three (types of) people whom Allah will neither speak to on the Day of Resurrection nor will He purify them (i.e., from their sins), nor will look upon them; and they will have a painful chastisement.

These are: An old man who commits fornication; a king who is a great liar and a poor man who is proud."

Source: Riyad As-Saliheen 1852 Grade: Sahih

Narrated Abu Huraira:

Allah's Messenger (ﷺ) said, "While I was sleeping, I was given the treasures of the earth and two gold bangles were put in my hands, and I did not like that, but I received the inspiration that I should blow on them, and I did so, and both of them vanished. I interpreted it as referring to the two liars between whom I am present; the ruler of Sana and the Ruler of Yamaha."

Source: Sahih Bukhari 4375

Mu'awiyah ibn Jaydah Qushayri said:

The Messenger of Allah (ﷺ) said:

"Woe to him who tells things, speaking falsely, to make people laugh thereby.

Woe to him! Woe to him!"

Source: Sunan Abu Dawood 4990
Grade: Hasan

Narrated `Aisha:

Some people asked Allah's Messenger (ﷺ) about the fortune-tellers. Allah's Messenger

(ﷺ) said to them, "They are nothing (i.e., liars)." The people said, 'O Allah's Messenger (ﷺ)! Sometimes they tell something which comes out to be true." Allah's Messenger (ﷺ) said, "That word which comes to be true is what a jinn snatches away by stealing and then pours it in the ear of his fortune-teller with a sound similar to the cackle of a hen, and then they add to it one-hundred lies."*

Source: Sahih Bukhari 6213

Abdur-Rahman bin Abi Laila said:

When `Ali bin Abi Talib heard the mu`addhin giving the adhan, he used to repeat after him. When he said, I bear witness that there is no god but Allah and I bear witness that Muhammad is the Messenger of Allah (ﷺ), `Ali would say: I bear witness that there is no god but Allah and I bear witness that Muhammad is the

Messenger of Allah (ﷺ), and that those who disbelieve Muhammad are the liars.

Source: Musnad Ahmad 965 Grade: Daif

It was narrated from Mu'awiyah that:

The Messenger of Allah forbade giving a false impression, and the false impression of a woman when she adds extra hair to her head.

Source: Sunan Nasai 5248 Grade: Sahih

Narrated Aisha:

(The wife of the Prophet) Whenever Allah's Messenger (ﷺ) intended to go on a journey, he used to draw lots among his wives and would take with him the one on whom the lot had fallen. Once he drew lots when he wanted to carry out a Battle, and the lot came upon me. So I proceeded with Allah's Messenger after Allah's order of veiling (the women) had been revealed and thus I was

carried in my howdah (on a camel) and dismounted while still in it. We carried on our journey, and when Allah's Messenger had finished his Battle and returned and we approached Medina, Allah's Messenger (ﷺ) ordered to proceed at night. When the army was ordered to resume the homeward journey, I got up and walked on till I left the army (camp) behind. When I had answered the call of nature, I went towards my howdah, but behold ! A necklace of mine made of Jaz Azfar (a kind of black bead) was broken and I looked for it and my search for it detained me. The group of people who used to carry me, came and carried my howdah on to the back of my camel on which I was riding, considering that I was therein. At that time women were light in weight and were not fleshy for they used to eat little (food), so those people did not feel the lightness of the howdah while raising it up, and I was still a young lady. They drove *away the camel and proceeded. Then I found my necklace after the army had gone. I came to their camp but found nobody therein so I went to the place where I used to stay, thinking that they would miss me and come back in my search. While I was sitting at my place, I felt sleepy and slept.*

Safwan bin Al-Mu'attil As-Sulami Adh-Dhakw-ani was behind the army. He had started in the last part of the night and reached my stationing place in the morning and saw the figure of a sleeping person. He came to me and recognized me on seeing me for he used to see me before veiling. I got up because of his saying: "Inna Li l-lahi wa inna ilaihi rajiun," (To Allah we belong and to Allah return) which he uttered on recognizing me. I covered my face with my garment, and by Allah, he did not say to me a single word except, "Inna Li l-lahi wa inna ilaihi rajiun," till he made his she-camel

*kneel down whereupon he trod on its
forelegs and I mounted it. Then Safwan set
out, leading the she-camel that was carrying
me, till we met the army while they were
resting during the hot midday. Then
whoever was meant for destruction, fell in
destruction, and the leader of the Ifk (forged
statement) was `Abdullah bin Ubai bin
Salul. After this we arrived at Medina and I
became ill for one month while the people
were spreading the forged statements of the
people of the Ifk, and I was not aware of
anything thereof.*

*But what aroused my doubt while I was
sick, was that I was no longer receiving from
Allah's Messenger (ﷺ) the same kindness as
I used to receive when I fell sick. Allah's
Messenger (ﷺ) would enter upon me, say a
greeting and add, "How is that (lady)?" and
then depart. That aroused my suspicion but
I was not aware of the propagated evil till I*

recovered from my ailment. I went out with
Um Mistah to answer the call of nature
towards Al-Manasi, the place where we used
to relieve ourselves, and used not to go out
for this purpose except from night to night,
and that was before we had lavatories close
to our houses. And this habit of ours was
similar to the habit of the old 'Arabs (in the
deserts or in the tents) concerning the
evacuation of the bowels, for we considered
it troublesome and harmful to take lavatories
in the houses. So I went out with Um
Mistah who was the daughter of Abi Ruhm
bin `Abd Manaf, and her mother was
daughter of Sakhr bin Amir who was the
aunt of Abi Bakr As-Siddiq, and her son was
Mistah bin Uthatha. When we had finished
our affair, Um Mistah and I came back
towards my house. Um Mistah stumbled
over her robe whereupon she said, "Let
Mistah be ruined! " I said to her, "What a
bad word you have said! Do you abuse a

man who has taken part in the Battle of Badr?' She said, "O you there! Didn't you hear what he has said?" I said, "And what did he say?" She then told me the statement of the people of the Ifk (forged statement) which added to my ailment. When I returned home, Allah's Messenger (ﷺ) came to me, and after greeting, he said, "How is that (lady)?" I said, "Will you allow me to go to my parents?" At that time I intended to be sure of the news through them.

Allah's Messenger (ﷺ) allowed me and I went to my parents and asked my mother, "O my mother! What are the people talking about?" My mother said, "O my daughter! Take it easy, for by Allah, there is no charming lady who is loved by her husband who has other wives as well, but that those wives would find fault with her." I said, "Subhan Allah! (Glory be to Allah!) Did the people really talk about that?" That night I kept on weeping the whole night till the morning. My tears never stopped, nor did I sleep, and morning broke while I was still weeping, Allah's Messenger (ﷺ) called `Ali bin Abi Talib and Usama bin Zaid when the Divine Inspiration delayed, in order to consult them as to the idea of divorcing his wife.

Usama bin Zaid told Allah's Messenger (ﷺ) of what he knew about the innocence of his wife and of his affection he kept for her. He said, "O Allah's Messenger (ﷺ)! She is your wife, and we do not know anything about her except good." But `Ali bin Abi Talib said, "O Allah's Messenger (ﷺ)! Allah does not impose restrictions on you; and there are plenty of women other than her. If you however, ask (her) slave girl, she will tell you the truth."

Aisha added: So Allah's Messenger (ﷺ) called for Barira and said, "O Barira! Did *you ever see anything which might have aroused your suspicion? (as regards Aisha). Barira said, "By Allah Who has sent you with the truth, I have never seen anything regarding Aisha which I would blame her for except that she is a girl of immature age who sometimes sleeps and leaves the dough of her family unprotected so that the domestic goats come and eat it." So Allah's Messenger (ﷺ) got up (and addressed) the people and asked for somebody who would take revenge on `Abdullah bin Ubai bin Salul then. Allah's Messenger (ﷺ), while on the pulpit, said, "O Muslims! Who will help me against a man who has hurt me by slandering my family? By Allah, I know nothing except good about my family, and people have blamed a man of whom I know nothing except good, and he never used to visit my family except with me,"*

*Sa`d bin Mu`adh Al-Ansari got up and said,
"O Allah's Messenger (ﷺ)! By Allah, I will
relieve you from him. If he be from the tribe
of (Bani) Al-Aus, then I will chop his head
off; and if he be from our brethren, the
Khazraj, then you give us your order and we
will obey it." On that, Sa`d bin 'Ubada got
up, and he was the chief of the Khazraj, and
before this incident he had been a pious man
but he was incited by his zeal for his tribe.
He said to Sa`d (bin Mu`adh), "By Allah the
Eternal, you have told a lie! You shall not
kill him and you will never be able to kill
him!" On that, Usaid bin Hudair, the
cousin of Sa`d (bin Mu`adh) got up and said
to Sa`d bin 'Ubada, "You are a liar! By
Allah the Eternal, we will surely kill him;
and you are a hypocrite defending the
hypocrites!" So the two tribes of Al-Aus and
Al-Khazraj got excited till they were on the
point of fighting with each other while
Allah's Messenger (ﷺ) was standing on the*

pulpit. Allah's Messenger (ﷺ) continued quietening them till they became silent whereupon he became silent too.

On that day I kept on weeping so much that neither did my tears stop, nor could I sleep. In the morning my parents were with me, and I had wept for two nights and a day without sleeping and with incessant tears till they thought that my liver would burst with weeping. While they were with me and I was weeping, an Ansari woman asked permission to see me. I admitted her and she sat and started weeping with me. While I was in that state, Allah's Messenger came to us, greeted, and sat down. He had never sat with me since the day what was said, was said. He had stayed a month without receiving any Divine Inspiration concerning my case. Allah's Messenger (ﷺ) recited the Tashahhud after he had sat down, and then said, "Thereafter, O `Aisha! I have been *informed such and-such a thing about you; and if you are innocent, Allah will reveal your innocence, and if you have committed a sin, then ask for Allah's forgiveness and repent to Him, for when a slave confesses his sin and then repents to Allah, Allah accepts his repentance." When Allah's Messenger had finished his speech, my tears ceased completely so that I no longer felt even a drop thereof.*

Then I said to my father, "Reply to Allah's Messenger (ﷺ) on my behalf as to what he said." He said, "By Allah, I do not know what to say to Allah's Messenger (ﷺ)." Then I said to my mother, "Reply to Allah's Messenger." She said, "I do not know what to say to Allah's Messenger (ﷺ)."

Still a young girl as I was and though I had little knowledge of Qur'an, I said, "By Allah, I know that you heard this story (of the Ifk) so much so that it has been planted

*in your minds and you have believed it. So
now, if I tell you that I am innocent, and
Allah knows that I am innocent, you will
not believe me; and if I confess something,
and Allah knows that I am innocent of it,
you will believe me. By Allah, I cannot find
of you an example except that of Joseph's
father: "So (for me) patience is most fitting
against that which you assert and it is Allah
(Alone) Whose help can be sought. Then I
turned away and lay on my bed, and at that
time I knew that I was innocent and that
Allah would reveal my innocence. But by
Allah, I never thought that Allah would sent
down about my affair, Divine Inspiration
that would be recited (forever), as I
considered myself too unworthy to be talked
of by Allah with something that was to be
recited: but I hoped that Allah's Messenger
(ﷺ) might have a vision in which Allah
would prove my innocence.*

*By Allah, Allah's Messenger (ﷺ) had not
left his seat and nobody had left the house
when the Divine Inspiration came to Allah's
Messenger (ﷺ) . So there overtook him the
same hard condition which used to overtake
him (when he was Divinely Inspired) so that
the drops of his sweat were running down,
like pearls, though it was a (cold) winter
day, and that was because of the heaviness of
the Statement which was revealed to him.
When that state of Allah's Messenger (ﷺ)
was over, and he was smiling when he was
relieved, the first word he said was, "Aisha,
Allah has declared your innocence." My
mother said to me, "Get up and go to him."*

*I said, "By Allah, I will not go to him and I
will not thank anybody but Allah."*

*So Allah revealed: "Indeed, those who came
with falsehood are a group among you. Do
not think it bad for you; rather it is good for
you. For every person among them is what*

[punishment] he has earned from the sin, and he who took upon himself the greater portion thereof - for him is a great punishment. (11) Why, when you heard it, did not the believing men and believing women think good of one another and say, "This is an obvious falsehood"? (12) Why did they [who slandered] not produce for it four witnesses? And when they do not produce the witnesses, then it is they, in the sight of Allah, who are the liars. (13) And if it had not been for the favor of Allah upon you and His mercy in this world and the Hereafter, you would have been touched for that [lie] in which you were involved by a great punishment (14) When you received it with your tongues and said with your mouths that of which you had no knowledge and thought it was insignificant while it was, in the sight of Allah, tremendous. (15) And why, when you heard it, did you not say, "It is not for us to speak of this.

Exalted are You, [O Allah]; this is a great slander"? (16) Allah warns you against returning to the likes of this [conduct], ever, if you should be believers. (17) And Allah makes clear to you the verses, and Allah is Knowing and Wise. (18) Indeed, those who like that immorality should be spread [or publicized] among those who have believed will have a painful punishment in this world and the Hereafter. And Allah knows and you do not know. (19) And if it had not been for the favor of Allah upon you and His mercy... and because Allah is Kind and Merciful. (20) (Quran verses 24:11-20).

When Allah revealed this to confirm my innocence, Abu Bakr As-Siddiq who used to provide for Mistah because of the latter's kinship to him and his poverty, said, "By Allah, I will never provide for Mistah anything after what he has said about Aisha".

So Allah revealed: "Let not those among you who are good and are wealthy swear not to give (help) to their kinsmen, those in need, and those who have left their homes for Allah's Cause. Let them Pardon and forgive (i.e. do not punish them). Do you not love that Allah should forgive you? Verily Allah is Oft-forgiving. Most Merciful." (24.22)

Abu Bakr said, "Yes, by Allah, I wish that Allah should forgive me." So he resumed giving Mistah the aid he used to give him before and said, "By Allah, I will never withhold it from him at all."

Aisha further said: Allah's Messenger (ﷺ) also asked Zainab bint Jahsh about my case. He said, "O Zainab! What have you seen?" She replied, "O Allah's Messenger (ﷺ)! I protect my hearing and my sight (by refraining from telling lies). I know nothing but good (about Aisha)." Of all the wives of Allah's Messenger (ﷺ), it was Zainab who aspired to receive from him the same favor as I used to receive, yet, Allah saved her (from telling lies) because of her piety. But her sister, Hamna, kept on fighting on her behalf so she was destroyed as were those who invented and spread the slander."

Source: Sahih Bukhari 4750

Narrated Abdullah bin Masood:

Allah's Messenger (ﷺ) entered Mecca (in the year of the Conquest) and there were three-hundred and sixty idols around the Ka`ba. He then started hitting them with a stick in his hand and say: 'Truth (i.e. Islam) has come and falsehood (disbelief) vanished. Truly falsehood (disbelief) is ever bound to vanish.' (17.81) 'Truth has come and falsehood (Iblis) can not create anything.' (34.49)

Source: Sahih Bukhari 4720

Asma' reported that a woman came to Allah's Messenger (ﷺ) and said:

I have a co-wife. Is there any harm for me if I give her the false impression (of getting something from my husband which he has not in fact given me)? Thereupon Allah's Messenger (ﷺ) said: The one who creates such a (false impression) of receiving what one has not been given is like one who wears the garment of falsehood.

Source: Sahih Muslim 2130a

Abu Bakrah reported:

The Messenger of Allah (ﷺ) said, "Shall I not inform you of one of the gravest of the cardinal sins?" We said: "Yes, O Messenger of Allah!" He (ﷺ) said, "To join others as partners with Allah in worship and to be undutiful to one's parents." The Messenger of Allah (ﷺ) sat up from his reclining position (in order to stress the importance of what he was going to say) and added, "I warn you making a false statement and giving a false testimony. I warn you against making a false statement and giving a false testimony." The Messenger of Allah (ﷺ) kept on repeating this (warning) till we wished he should stop.

Source: Riyad as-Salihin 1550 Grade: Sahih

Narrated Anas bin Malik:

The Prophet (ﷺ) said, "The biggest of Al-Ka`ba'ir (the great sins) are (1) to join others as partners in worship with Allah, (2) to murder a human being, (3) to be undutiful to one's parents (4) and to make a false statement," or said, "to give a false witness."

Source: Sahih Bukhari 6871

Ayman bin Khuraim said the Prophet stood giving a Khutbah saying:

"O you people False witness is tantamount to Shirk(polytheism) with Allah" Then the Messenger of Allah recited: So shun the Rijs of the idols, and shun false speech.

Source: Jami` at-Tirmidhi 2299 Grade: Daif

Wathilah bin Al-Asqa' reported:

The Messenger of Allah (ﷺ) said, "Of the worst lies are: to claim a false father, or to pretend to have seen what one has not seen (tell a false dream), or to attribute to the Messenger of Allah what he has not said."

Source: Riyad as-Salihin 843 Grade: Sahih

Narrated Imran ibn Husayn:

The Prophet (ﷺ) said: If anyone swears a false oath in confinement, he should make his seat in Hell on account of his (act).

Source: Sunan Abi Dawud 3242 Grade: Sahih

It was narrated from Ibn 'Umar that the Messenger of Allah (ﷺ) said:

'The one who bears false witness will not move away (on the Day of Resurrection) until Allah condemns him to Hell.' "

Source: Sunan Ibn Majah 2373 Grade: Daif

Abu Hurairah narrated that :

the Prophet said: "Whoever does not leave false speech, and acting according to it, then Allah is not in any need of him leaving his food and his drink.(fasting)"

Source: Jami Tirmidhi 707 Grade: Sahih

It was narrated from Ibn 'Abbas that the Messenger of Allah (ﷺ) said:

"Whoever tells of a false dream, will be ordered (on the Day of Resurrection) to tie two grains of barley together, and he will be punished for that."

Source: Sunan Ibn Majah 3916 Grade: Sahih

It was narrated that Qais bin Abi Gharazah said:

"The Prophet came to us when we were in the marketplace and said: 'This marketplace is filled with idle talk and (false) oaths, so mix some charity with it.'"

Source: Sunan an-Nasa'i 3799 Grade: Sahih

Jabir bin 'Abdullah reported the Messenger of Allah (ﷺ) said:

"Whoever swears a false oath near this pulpit of mine, let him take his place in Hell, even if it is for a green twig."

Source: Sunan Ibn Majah 2325 Grade:
Sahih

Asma' bint Yazid reported:

*"Food was brought to the Prophet and it
was presented before us. We said, "We do
not have an appetite for it." The Prophet
said, "Do not combine hunger with lies."*

Source: Sunan Ibn Mājah 3298 Grade:
Hasan

Narrated Abu Huraira:

*The Prophet (ﷺ) said, "(There are) three
(types of persons to whom) Allah will
neither speak to them on the Day of
Resurrections, nor look at them (They are):--
(1) a man who takes a false oath that he has
been offered for a commodity a price greater
than what he has actually been offered; (2)
and a man who takes a false oath after the
`Asr (prayer) in order to grab the property*

of a Muslim through it; (3) and a man who forbids others to use the remaining superfluous water. To such a man Allah will say on the Day of Resurrection, 'Today I withhold My Blessings from you as you withheld the superfluous part of that (water) which your hands did not create.' "

Source: Sahih Bukhari 7446

Al-Hasan bin 'Ali said:

"I remember that the Messenger of Allah said: 'Leave what makes you in doubt for what does not make you in doubt. The truth brings tranquility while falsehood sows doubt.'"

Source: Jami Tirmidhi 2518 Grade: Sahih

It was narrated from Abu Dharr that the Prophet said:

"There are three to whom Allah will not speak on the Day of Resurrection, or look at them, or sanctify them, and theirs will be a painful torment." The Messenger of Allah repeated (three times) and Abu Dharr said: "May they be lost and doomed."

He(the Prophet) said: "The one(of males) who lets his garment hang beneath his ankles, a vendor who tries to sell his product by means of false oaths, and the one who reminds people of what he has given them."

Source: Sunan an-Nasa'i 2563 Grade: Sahih

Abdullah ibn 'Amr said:

"Abu Masood, what did you hear the Messenger of Allah say about 'People who make false claims?'"

He replied, "I heard him say, 'A bad mount for a man' and I heard him say, 'Cursing a believer is like killing him.'"

Source: Adab Mufrad 763 Grade: Sahih

It was narrated Anas bin Malik said:

"The Messenger of Allah (ﷺ) said: 'Whoever gives up telling lies in support of a false claim, a palace will be built for him in the outskirts of Paradise. Whoever gives up argument when he is in the right, a palace will be built from him in the middle (of Paradise). And whoever had good behavior, a palace will be built for him in the highest reaches (of Paradise).'"

Source: Sunan Ibn Majah 51 Grade: Hasan

It is reported on the authority of Hammam bin al-Harith that a man used to carry tales to the governor. We were sitting in the mosque.

the people said: He is one who carries tales to the governor. He (the narrator) said: Then he came and sat with us. Thereupon Hudhaifa remarked:

I heard the Messenger of Allah (ﷺ) saying: The bearer of false tales would never enter heaven.

Source: Sahih Muslim 105b

Jabir ibn 'Abdullah al-Ansari reported that the Prophet said:

"Whoever has a favor done for him should repay it. If he cannot find anything he can use to repay it, he should praise the one who did it. When he praises him, he thanks him. If he is silent, he is ungrateful to him. If someone adorns himself with something he has not been given, it is as if he was wearing a garment of lies."

Source: Adab Mufrad 215 Grade: Sahih

Malik narrated from al-Walid ibn Abdullah ibn Sayyad that al-Muttalib ibn Abdullah ibn Hantab al-Makhzumi informed him:

A man asked the Messenger of Allah, "What is backbiting?" The Messenger of Allah, said, "It is to mention about a man what he does not want to hear." He said, "Messenger of Allah! Even if it is true?" The Messenger of Allah, said, "If you utter something false, then it is slander."

Source: Muwatta Imam Malik

A'isha said Allah's messenger said:

"There are six whom I have cursed, whom I pray that God may curse, and every prophet's prayer is answered:

He who makes additions to God's Book,

he who declares God's destiny to be false,

he who rules proudly to exalt him whom God has humbled and humble him whom God has exalted,

he who profanes God's sacred area,

he who considers he may do to my family what God has declared forbidden,

and he who abandons my sunna."

Source: Mishkat al Masabih 109 Grade: Hasan

Narrated 'Abdullah bin 'Abdur-Rahman bin Abu Husain:

That the Messenger of Allah (ﷺ) said: "Indeed, Allah will surely admit three into Paradise by a single arrow. Its maker who seeks good by his making it, the one who shoots it, and the one who holds arrows for him." And he said: "Practice archery and practice riding, and the you should practice archery is more beloved to me than that you should ride. All idle pastimes that the Muslim man engages in are falsehood, except for his shooting of his bow, his training of his horse, and his playing with his wife, for they are from truth."

Source: Jami Tirmidhi 1637 Grade: Sahih

Narrated Ubada bin As-Samit:

I gave the pledge of allegiance to the Prophet (ﷺ) with a group of people, and he said, "I take your pledge that you will not worship anything besides Allah, will not steal, will not commit infanticide, will not slander others by forging false statements and spreading it, and will not disobey me in anything good. And whoever among you fulfill all these (obligations of the pledge), his reward is with Allah. And whoever commits any of the above crimes and receives his legal punishment in this world, that will be his expiation and purification. But if Allah screens his sin, it will be up to Allah, Who will either punish or forgive him according to His wish." Abu `Abdullah said: "If a thief repents after his hand has been cut off, the his witness well be accepted. Similarly, if any person upon whom any legal *punishment has been inflicted, repents, his witness will be accepted."*

Source: Sahih al-Bukhari 6801

Abū Hurairah said:

the Messenger of Allah ﷺ said, "A servant does not entirely have faith until he abandons lying even while joking, and abandons arguing even if he is correct."

Source: Musnad Ahmed 8630 Grade: Daif

Abu Hurairah reported:

The Prophet (ﷺ) said, "He who believes in Allah and the Last Day must either speak good or remain silent."

Source: Riyad As-Salihin 1511 Grade: Sahih

Narrated Ibn `Abbas:

The Prophet (ﷺ) said, "Allah said, 'The son of Adam tells a lie against me though he has no right to do so, and he abuses Me though he has no right to do so. As for his telling a lie against Me, it is that he claims that I cannot recreate him as I created him before; and as for his abusing Me, it is his statement that I have offspring. No! Glorified be Me! I am far from taking a wife or offspring.' "

Source: Sahih Bukhari 4482

Narrated Abu Sa`id Al-Khudri:

During the lifetime of the Prophet (ﷺ) some people said: O Allah's Messenger (ﷺ)! Shall we see our Lord on the Day of Resurrection?" The Prophet (ﷺ) said, "Yes; do you have any difficulty in seeing the sun at midday when it is bright and there is no cloud in the sky?" They replied, "No." He said, "Do you have any difficulty in seeing the moon on a full moon night when it is bright and there is no cloud in the sky?" They replied, "No." The Prophet (ﷺ) said, "(Similarly) you will have no difficulty in seeing Allah on the Day of

Resurrection as you have no difficulty in seeing either of them. On the Day of Resurrection, a call-maker will announce, "Let every nation follow that which they used to worship." Then none of those who used to worship anything other than Allah like idols and other deities but will fall in Hell (Fire), till there will remain none but those who used to worship Allah, both those who were obedient (i.e. good) and those who were disobedient (i.e. bad) and the remaining party of the people of the Scripture. Then the Jews will be called upon and it will be said to them, 'Who do you use to worship?' They will say, 'We used to worship Ezra, the son of Allah.' It will be said to them, 'You are liars, for Allah has never taken anyone as a wife or a son. What do you want now?' They will say, 'O our Lord! We are thirsty, so give us something to drink.' They will be directed and addressed thus, 'Will you drink,' whereupon they will be gathered unto Hell (Fire) which will look like a mirage whose different sides will be destroying each other. Then they will *fall into the Fire. Afterwards the Christians will be called upon and it will be said to them, 'Who do you use to worship?' They will say, 'We used to worship Jesus, the son of Allah.' It will be said to them, 'You are liars, for Allah has never taken anyone as a wife or a son,' Then it will be said to them, 'What do you want?' They will say what the former people have said. Then, when there remain (in the gathering) none but those who used to worship Allah (Alone, the real Lord of the Worlds) whether they were obedient or disobedient. Then (Allah) the Lord of the worlds will come to them in a shape nearest to the picture they had in their minds about Him. It will be said, 'What are you waiting for?' Every nation have followed what they used to worship.' They will reply, 'We left the people in the world when we were in great need of them and we did not take them as friends. Now we are waiting for our Lord Whom we used to worship.' Allah will say, 'I am your Lord.' They will say twice or thrice, 'We do not worship any besides Allah.'"*

Source: Sahih Bukhari 4581

Narrated Abu Huraira:

While the Prophet (ﷺ) was saying something in a gathering, a Bedouin came and asked him, "When would the Hour (Doomsday) take place?" Allah's Messenger (ﷺ) continued his talk, so some people said that Allah's Messenger (ﷺ) had heard the question, but did not like what that Bedouin had asked. Some of them said that Allah's Messenger (ﷺ) had not heard it. When the Prophet (ﷺ) finished his speech, he said, "Where is the questioner, who inquired about the Hour (Doomsday)?" The Bedouin said, "I am here, O Allah's Messenger ." Then the Prophet (ﷺ) said, "When honesty is lost, then wait for the Hour (Doomsday)." The Bedouin said, "How will that be lost?" The Prophet (ﷺ) said, "When the power or authority comes in the hands of unfit persons, then wait for the Hour."

Source: Sahih Bukhari 59

Abu Huraira reported:

The Messenger of Allah said:

"Verily, the first people to be judged on the Day of Resurrection will be a man who was martyred. He will be brought, the blessings of Allah will be made known, and he will acknowledge them. Allah will say: What did you do with them? The man will say: I fought in Your cause until I was martyred. Allah will say: You have lied, for you fought only that it would be said you were brave, thus it was said. Then, Allah will order him to be dragged upon his face until he is cast into Hellfire.

Another man studied religious knowledge, taught others, and recited the Quran. He will be brought, the blessings of Allah will be made known, and he will acknowledge them. Allah will say: What did you do with them? The man will say: I learned religious knowledge, taught others, and I recited the Quran for Your sake. Allah will say: You have lied, for you studied only that it would be said you are a scholar and you recited the Quran only that it would be said you are a reciter, thus it was said. Then, Allah will order him to be dragged upon his face until he is cast into Hellfire.

Another man was given an abundance of blessings from Allah and every kind of wealth. He will be brought, the blessings of Allah will be made known, and he will acknowledge them. Allah will say: What did you do with them? The man will say: I did not leave any good cause beloved to You but that I spent on it for Your sake. Allah will say: You have lied, for you spent only that it would be said you are generous, thus it was said. Then, Allah will order him to be dragged upon his face until he is cast into Hellfire."

Source: Sahih Muslim 1905